MY BUSINESS ATE
My Life
{A RECOVERY PLAN}

For entrepreneurs, solopreneurs, professionals, and corporate leaders.

My Business Ate My Life. Copyright © 2016 by Elizabeth Verwey.

All rights reserved. No part of this book may be used or reproduced in any manner whatsoever without written permission except in the case of brief quotations embodied in articles and reviews. For information, contact elizabeth@officementors.com

FIRST EDITION

Cover designed by Raymond Helkio

ISBN 978-0-9739542-3-4

Acknowledgments

I want to thank Bob Millard, my father, and first mentor. And, I'm grateful to my capable children, Michael and Corinne Verwey.

Behind every writer is a patient partner, and Ramsay is the guy who encourages me in any project I want to accomplish. Thank you for your ongoing support and love.

Anything is possible within a circle of support. I am fortunate to be part of several circles that elevate my level of thinking about the possibilities in this short life.

Special thanks to Peter Marmorek, and gratitude to each member of our treasured writing group. My inspirational business friends include James Braithwaite, Greg Dobson, Louie Katsis, Brian Kotoka, Larry Lychowyd and Jackie Porter. My cherished friends who have helped me in my journey include Kate Allen, Hazel Anderson, Nadia Bassett, Mike McEwan, Oriah Mountain Dreamer, Jennifer Murray, Tim Paulsen, Doug Payne, David Shelly, Lisa Spain, Karyn Spiesman, Janice Waugh, Scott White, Jim Woodbridge, Jim and Marney Winn.

Special thanks go out to a trio of editors, Lucille Blainey, Nina Munteanu and Cheryl Xavier. My heartfelt thanks go out to each one of you. Clearly, I could not have written this book without you.

Table of Contents
Preface
Introduction

1. Preparing the Menu or First Things First   16
- *a.* How to Use This Book   18
- *b.* Lifestyle Audit   20
- *c.* Do You Want to Recover?   24
- *d.* Differentiating *Self* and *Time* Management   27
- *e.* Templates Help You Plan   32
- *f.* Needs vs Wants   40
- *g.* Urgent vs Important   41
- *h.* Letting Go   42

2. Creating Your Own Recipe or Your Recovery Plan   45
- *a.* Time Management vs Self-Management   46
- *b.* Clarify Your Values   47
- *c.* Technology   50
- *d.* The 3 Ds: Delegating, Dovetailing, Deleting   51

3. Be the Head Chef or Getting and Staying Organized   59
- *a.* Organizing Your Physical Space   60
- *b.* How to Begin?   61
- *c.* Daily, Weekly, Monthly Organization   64
- *d.* Goal Charts   67
- *e.* Accountability   71
- *f.* Motivational Focus Program   72
- *g.* Personal vs Business   73

4. Menu Makeover for a Better Life or Completing Projects   75
- *a.* List All Your Projects   76
- *b.* Blocking Off Time   79
- *c.* Rewarding Yourself   80

5. Kitchen Help or Delegating and Staffing		82
a.	The Work Plan Makeover	83
b.	Test and Measure	86
c.	How to Delegate	87
d.	Staffing or Team Management Pointers	91
e.	Staffing or Team Models	93
6. Finding Your Perfect Recipe or Refining Your Recovery Plan		97
a.	Try Something New	98
b.	Test and Measure	100
c.	Refine Your Plan	101
d.	Your Personal Recovery Plan	102
e.	Annual Review	109
7. Adding Another Course or Expanding Your Business		111
a.	Hear a Need	112
b.	Streams of Income	113
c.	Taste Test	114
d.	Workshops/Events	116
e.	Business Plans as Living Documents	118
8. Reclaiming the Flavour of Life or Reclaiming Your Life		120
a.	Assessing NOW	121
b.	The Power of Play	122
c.	Boundaries with Others	122
d.	Add a Dash of Fun	124
e.	Finding Mentors	127
9. Bite-sized Treats or Treasured Moments		134
10. After Dinner Mint or Epilogue		148

— PREFACE —

Once upon a time, in a city by a lake, I woke up with a start to the realization that my business had consumed my life! I jumped out of bed and said out loud *"My business ate my life!"* In the next few weeks, I developed a recovery plan that would work for me.

How had I come to this place?

In 1990, I became director of new development for *Performers for Literacy*, a not-for-profit organization that created programs for families to glamourize and encourage reading and writing. Working with a committed group of actors, I helped grow this project into a national charity. It was an exciting time of live shows, fundraisers, storefronts and special events--all celebrating the message that reading is fun. I had a finger in each of these pies. What a privilege it was to be associated with this amazing group of people! Though I constantly bit off more than I could chew, the experience taught me how to juggle multiple tasks and time zones and prioritize wisely.

I learned the difference between urgent and important tasks. We began to write down our processes and was constantly assessing what needed to happen next. Although it took time away from daily operations to write an Operations Manual, it paid off in the long run, as it helped me take an objective view of what we were doing, and the manuals made it much easier to delegate work to key staff and volunteers.

I lived the African proverb: *"If you want to go fast, go alone; if you want to go far, go together."* The organization was able to spread the literacy message far and wide with the help of a handful of committed team members and hundreds of volunteers.

The phone drove me to work, from the first ring in the morning till the last at night. With six time zones in our country, spanning 4½ hours, work sure ate up my days! I fell asleep thinking about work and kept paper and pen by my bed to capture my great ideas or reminders during the night. Some of these still made sense in the light of day; others were nonsense.

Then, out of the blue, my big brother died of a heart attack at 50 years of age. Just 40 days earlier, we had celebrated his birthday with a family lobster feast. David was a firefighter who owned horses, and he was my hero. He was 13 years older than I, and my real life guardian angel. He took care of me through childhood illnesses and protected me through some rough teen years. It was devastating to lose him, and in my grief, I did not want to work. I wanted the world to stop and let me catch up on my personal life.

I only wanted to connect with the people I valued in my life. Clearly, I could see that I was working too hard. Yet, when I was with the people I valued, I felt an internal pressure to go back to work.

I started to recognize that I was a workaholic. I thrived on my accomplishments and sought the adrenaline rush of doing way too much. It was tough to say "no" to any offer. I thought about work all the time, even when I had decided not to, and I couldn't see how to change my ways.

I wrote a list of personal goals to accomplish before I turned 50. It seemed important, just in case I died of a heart attack like my big brother did. The first thing on that list was a family vacation. I decided that as a family, we needed to go away to create time to reconnect. We pulled out all the stops and planned a European adventure with our children. The Board of Directors didn't want me to leave. Still, I let them know that I'd need to resign for a month that summer, and if my job was open when I returned, I'd take it.

We travelled to four countries in five weeks. It was a bonding experience. We happily explored new landscapes together, visited relatives in Holland, and took a magical carriage tour in Belgium. We re-lived history as we took the ferry into the White Cliffs of Dover and 'lived' in a castle in the New Forest in England. We walked around Stonehenge and saw a tank crossing. I recalled my father saying he had crossed in a tank during WWII. We visited Windsor Castle in London and Speaker's Corners. We delighted in seeing European museums and the Louvre in Paris and we fed the pigeons in Trafalgar Square in London, just like Mary Poppins!

I learned that it was time to have more fun. I decided to become a 'workafrolic'! I'd squeeze more fun into my life. At Performers for Literacy, I replaced myself with a new staff member. Now that she was working 40 hours a week, I was able to work part-time. Freeing up my time opened my eyes to new options. It was time to move on to launch a new business with my personal goals in mind. I would show people how to grow their business, they would do the work, and my family could still go on holiday!

My new business played to my strength, which is helping business owners find a better balance between work and home. A brainstorming session with a good friend helped me clarify my business offer. My focus would be Space, Time, and Balance. Once clients got these three factors in order, they could grow their business with my support. In doing so, I'd also help myself create the life I really wanted to live.

Soon after, I started earning accolades: two business awards, 'Best New Market Niche' and 'Home-Based Business of the Year' from my local Business Development Centre; and another award from the City of Toronto. But the real reward has been the satisfaction of helping people reclaim their lives.

Since 1998, I've helped over a thousand business owners become more efficient and effective and live a little happier as well.

--- POSTSCRIPT ---

As for me personally, I passed the 50 mark in fine health. I had accomplished most of the things important to me on my list, from designing and planting awesome gardens in my home, to writing articles for business newspapers and magazines. As my son was completing his Master's thesis, I published my first book, *The Mentors Circle* and started speaking to groups of entrepreneurs. Stretching myself even more, I created fundraisers for my favorite charities: a duct tape sculpture competition and a photo scavenger hunt. I even shaved my head to raise more money for charity. The CN Tower was my Mount Everest and I climbed its 1,700+ steps to raise funds for another charity. Now, I don't want any excuse to hold me back. I wrote up a new list–of the fears that no longer served me. After all, anything's possible while you are still alive.

Client Story

A Corporate Trainer toiled away into the wee hours of each morning in his home office. He'd fall into bed around 2 am and set the alarm for 8 am to start all over again. He brought me in to help him carve out some time for his family.
We started by identifying which work he could outsource

to a virtual assistant. We established standing orders for some of his training materials and automated many of his other routine chores. This bought him some sleep and one evening per week with his family.

At our second meeting, I asked him about the photos of golf courses on his wall. He told me that before his business gobbled up all his time, he had been an avid golfer. I learned that he was currently only golfing at charity events. Through brainstorming, he decided that he would begin golfing once per week. He felt sure that this would build his network. When we reconnected a month later, I was delighted to discover that he had invited his sons and a nephew to replace his corporate buddies on the golf course. His wife appreciated the break and that he had established a standing date night with her: an idea that he had initially rejected as being too predictable.

INTRODUCTION

How will this book help you? I want to inspire you by sharing my own experience and a few client stories to help you gain a better balance between your personal and professional life. I will guide you to set realistic goals and celebrate each achievement as you consider your own recovery process.

Remember when you learned to drive a car? If you were lucky enough to take lessons, the instructor trained you to scan blocks ahead to monitor what was coming towards you. This book will help business owners take the same long view.

The thesis of this book is simple: getting better control of your work space and time will help you grow your business and enjoy a better balance in your life.

Have you caught yourself watching the bumper ahead of you while you stew over your current business challenges? Or noticed that the steering wheel has started pulling to the left and realized you need your alignment checked? The ideas presented in this book help you take a step back to see the big picture. You'll learn to deal with short-term issues as they happen, all the while keeping your focus on your long-term goals.

Business owners too often focus on making money. The more successful you become, the more you can get stuck in the 'making money mode.' By the time you have enough money, you don't have time to use it, as you're still doing everything yourself! At that point, you may ponder, "do I own the business or does the business own me?"

You begin spending money to 'buy back' bits of time. This might mean that someone cleans for you, while another person prepares your meals, or you have a rich mix of staff or sub-contractors working for you.

Take time to stand back and view the big picture. Once you put a few administrative, support or control systems in place, you can pull away from the daily grind, consider your options and make decisions that support you in doing more of what you enjoy.

You may want to use the services of a virtual assistant or a bookkeeper. If you enjoy cooking, you might order your groceries online so you can have more time to prepare food. Or, if you don't enjoy cooking, use a meal delivery service to start eating better. After you have some extra time to think, it becomes possible to identify ways to build some passive income into your business. Imagine taking a few days off while still making money! It all begins by gathering the information you need to make some small changes that save you time and money.

You'll identify which changes best suit your style and develop new habits, one at a time. Once these modifications are in place, you'll be able to reclaim or enhance parts of your life.

I've written this book as a 'banquet of ideas' so you can choose options that suit your situation. There are no "wrong" choices. Taste-test a few of these ideas and you may find that you carve out some 'extra' time for yourself.

Client Story

A manufacturer of Celtic garden products was a creative individual who did not have strong sales skills. At our first two meetings, we established distinct 'zones' in her manufacturing process. We prepared for an increase in orders.

We outlined a process for each 'zone.' With my support, she approached several agents to sell her line. She was successful in finding an agent who sold a ton of her products. We then found a co-op student who was interested in doing this type of work. Soon she had a nest egg in the bank, and was able to hire an employee to fulfill orders while she designed the next line of products. The next co-op student took over her shipping desk and suggested some improvements.

Don't waste this time!

Sign up for that course you've always wanted to take or set up a weekly "walk and talk" with a neighbor or friend. You will begin to leave your work behind and build in some time for yourself. I hope you will choose to replace your busyness with some **'treasured moments'**—whether that's lounging around in a hammock, going to a concert, joining a hula hoop class or sharing a progressive dinner with friends. Or try out some of my favourite treasured moments, which I have shared at the end of this book.

Client Story

An entrepreneur in recovery services worked with me over ten months to grow his dream business. At our first meeting, our goal was to reclaim his week-ends. He was working 'in the business' of counselling Monday to Friday, and 'on the business' each week-end, preparing invoices and paying bills.

He rented space in a doctor's office. At our first meeting, we dealt with his urgent need to reclaim some personal time. As I prepared to leave that appointment, I asked him to tell me about his dreams for his business. He described a group practice that would be relatively easy to build. He was surprised to learn that I felt certain that we could establish that dream in under a year. We met each month and he took the necessary steps, one at a time. He currently oversees a practice that has five counsellors and other part-time contractors. They have a posh reception area, five offices and three group rooms that are booked by counsellors and other groups. His net |expenses are about the same as he was paying as a solopreneur, but he has more income and flexibility. He has built in some passive income, works part-time and is able to travel regularly.

Don't bite off more than you can chew!

A recovery plan is a process. Select new habits that are a good fit for you and your business. Brainstorm ideas with a trusted friend; consider your options and get the support you need to take it one step at a time; focus on developing one new habit at a time. If you aim to add only one new habit per month, you will feel less resistance to your recovery plan.

When making significant changes in life, I am reminded of the kid's joke.
> *Question: How do you eat an elephant?*
> *Answer: One bite at a time.*

Choose one bite. Chew on it awhile. Consider the whole buffet, and sample another item. Try something new. Just a taste. You may find that you like it. My hope is that you will gather new ideas and information to re-envision your life in a more self-fulfilling light. You will, in time, find the balance that feels right to you. An added bonus is discovering simple pleasures along the way.

Remember, your recovery plan is not a one-shot fix. Some adjustments are only short term. Like driving your car, one day you notice your steering wheel starting to shake and you know you need your wheels balanced. When I find myself feeling off-balance in that 'pressure cooker' routine again, I review my recovery plan and take the necessary steps to get my business and personal life back on track. I know this recovery strategy works. I've done it.

Enough already!
Let's get into the kitchen and start cooking!

CHAPTER 1

Preparing the Menu or First Things First

    a. How to Use This Book
    b. Lifestyle Audit
    c. Do You Want to Recover?
    d. Differentiate *Self* and *Time* Management
    e. Templates Can Work
    f. Needs vs Wants
    g. Urgent vs Important
    h. Letting Go

My Business Ate *My Life*

Chapter 1
Preparing the Menu or First Things First

Are you feeling overwhelmed by your work, business or life in general? Are you ready to see beyond your own vision? People invite me into their business when they realize that something is 'off kilter.' They used to love what they do and then they hit a tipping point, but they can't remember when or how it happened.

I understand. I've been there. It's a bit like reading a book by a window at dusk. When you're engrossed in the book, you don't notice that the light is getting dimmer. All of a sudden, you feel your eyes straining and look up to realize how dark the room has become. You know exactly what to do. You rub your eyes and turn on the light.

It's not as easy when you're busy running a business. That's why I wrote this book. When you wake up to the fact that you're working way too hard, you need to get your bearings quickly. Where do you turn? What do you do first?

Since 1998, more than a thousand business owners have employed the ideas I've included in this book and have gone on to become more effective and efficient in their business practices.

My goal is to guide you to grow your business and carve out time to enjoy your life. Do you want to make more money or have more time available to you? These options are not mutually exclusive. Seemingly small changes, from developing new habits or streamlining your processes to hiring or delegating to capable people, can make a huge difference.

This approach has worked with remarkable results for solopreneurs, entrepreneurs with from 2 to 50 staff, SMEs (Small and medium-sized enterprises), corporate climbers and professionals.

It's worked for presidents, COOs, managers, lawyers, not-for-profits and charities. It's worked in diverse industries from manufacturing and retail to health care and professional services.

And it can work for you. Even if you're too busy to read a whole book on the subject of reorganizing your life!

a) How to use this book

Our focus is the WIN Principle: W.I.N. is an acronym for **W**hat's **I**mportant **N**ow?

The 'Lifestyle Audit' (page 18) functions as a map or GPS to help you identify your specific challenges and guide you to the chapters in this book that target these areas specifically.

Taking the 'Lifestyle Audit' will enable you to pinpoint where to begin reading to meet your most urgent needs.

We are creatures of habit and it takes us time to develop new skills to change our lives. It's much easier when we pair our new habits with ones that are already established.

Skim those chapters that the 'Lifestyle Audit' leads you to and choose one or two ideas that you relate to right away. Try them out. Once you have a few wins, review some of the other ideas. They may feel more manageable once you have already gained some ground.

Small changes can make a big difference in how you live your life. For example, let's look at your Digital Manners. Do you reply to texts and e-mails while other people are speaking to you? Say it ain't so! If it is, this could be your first step. Put down the phone or turn away from the computer when someone speaks to you. Listen to them, and reply to texts and e-mails later. It will deepen both experiences. You may try making the bedroom a digital-free zone (no cell phones, iPads, computers, TV, etc.). It's a huge step forward that will improve other areas of your life, like sleep hygiene, intimacy with your partner, and so on. After you've made that a habit, you may even want to try eating your meals free of digital distractions.

Use the goal chart in this book to choose your goals and the specific steps you want to take. Work on one area at a time. Business? Relationships? Family? Treat this book as a 'choose your own adventure' experience.

You'll find many quick, accessible ideas in these pages. For example, taking 'Micro-vacations' can help you return to your business and life refreshed and recharged.

Making time for more 'Treasured Moments' will shift your energy quickly and help you uncover more fun as you become more effective in your business.

The last thing I ask you to consider as you begin taming your business and reclaiming your life is, who do you know who might support your efforts? This person may even want to join you on this journey. Lifestyle changes are always easier when using the buddy system. It does not matter if you plan to reduce your weight, stop drinking, or tame your business. Making life changes is easier with a support system.

b) *Lifestyle Audit – My Business Ate My Life*

To find your personal starting point, check off YES or NO for each question in every section. There is no pass/fail on this quiz. You know yourself best. Your responses will simply guide you to where to begin your recovery journey.

Getting Started

	YES	NO
Do I know the difference between urgent and important?	____	____
Do I work on important activities as often as I want to?	____	____
Do I want to reclaim a personal life?	____	____
Do I spend the time I want with family and friends?	____	____
Do I have two close friendships?	____	____
TOTALS	____	____

Getting Organized

	YES	NO
Do I know what's in my file drawers?	____	____
Am I clear about what needs to be done?	____	____
Do I write out my weekly or monthly goals?	____	____
Do I feel ready to make a change?	____	____
Do I reward myself for getting things done?	____	____
Do I work the hours that I plan to work?	____	____
TOTALS	____	____

Delegating & Staffing

	YES	NO
Have I been on a real vacation in the last two years?	____	____
Does my business make money while I'm away?	____	____
Do I have support from staff or volunteers?	____	____
Am I open to new ideas to get more done?	____	____
Do I have a hobby or leisure activity that I enjoy?	____	____
TOTALS	____	____

Expanding Your Business

	YES	NO
Is my business where I want it to be?	_____	_____
Do I have a business plan for the next two years?	_____	_____
Do I have one or more mentors for my business?	_____	_____
TOTALS	_____	_____

Surviving Your Business

	YES	NO
Do I weigh what I want to weigh?	_____	_____
Do I get enough exercise?	_____	_____
Do I have regular medical checkups?	_____	_____
Do I seek answers to my health challenges?	_____	_____
Do I have a spiritual or religious practice?	_____	_____
TOTALS	_____	_____

Summarize your YES and NO answers below for each of the above sections to learn where to find specific information to address your most pressing needs. You will benefit by reading the whole book, but you can jump right into the information you need right now.

Remember, we're going to use the W.I.N. (What's Important Now) principle.

Getting Started

Total number of YES answers   _____

Total number of NO answers   _____

Chapters 1 and 2 help you identify your own reasons to shift your habits and offer more than a dozen ideas to consider as you move away from working too hard, towards your more harmonious life.

Getting Organized

Total number of YES answers _____

Total number of NO answers _____

Chapters 3 and 4 guide you to organize your space, your time, and how to reach your goals. You will find some practical ways to make significant progress. You also plan how to reward yourself for reaching your goals.

Delegating and Staffing

Total number of YES answers _____

Total number of NO answers _____

Chapters 5 and 6 provide tips and tricks of great delegation. There are many ways to develop a virtual team to support you create more time for yourself. You will develop your personal recovery plan and find an annual review that will help in the future.

Expanding Your Business

Total number of YES answers _____

Total number of NO answers _____

Chapters 7 and 8 give insights into how to hear a need and add streams of income to your business. There are some marketing ideas that will help you and you will learn new ways to find new mentors.

Surviving Your Business

Total number of YES answers   _____

Total number of NO answers   _____

Making your health a priority is so important that every chapter in this book includes ways to protect and improve your wellbeing. You are the biggest asset in your business! Take care of yourself.

Be sure to read the 'Treasured Moments' in chapter 9 to find inspiration to fit more fun into the extra bits of time you discover. Enjoy the journey of reclaiming more life in your days. Chapter 10 outlines how running a business is a little like body surfing!

Add up the number of your YES answers and your NO answers for each audit section. This is not a test. You are the pilot of your own life. Review your NO answers to help you identify which areas need attention. Which ones are urgent? Use the W.I.N. (What's Important Now) Principle to choose your top three concerns. Tackle them first.

In which audit sections are your most important NOs?

Which chapters address those concerns in detail? Make this your journey towards your YES—one step at a time.

Read these chapters first to find some quick W.I.N.'s. They will energize you to try other ideas later to achieve the lifestyle you desire. You may need to say NO to something else to open up time for your YES. You will gather information and make decisions that will lead you to your new and improved lifestyle. It's easier to move toward YES when you bring awareness to the end result. In other words, when you 'Yearn Each Success' (Y.E.S.).

As you read this book, you will find tips and fresh ideas that will support you in getting closer to the Y.E.S. lifestyle you desire.

No matter where you begin, read the 'Treasured Moments' for inspiration to fit more fun into the extra bits of time you will discover.

But now, before we begin, it's important for you to ask yourself this tough question:

c) Do You Want to Recover?

This question must be asked. Particularly if other people in your life want you to free up more time for them. Think about whether you want more time for yourself or others.

Some clients I know are so unhappy with their personal lives that it's easier for them to work all the time. In that way, they don't have to deal with loneliness or unpleasant family situations by not being present. They may end up losing friends and family connections because they neglect to foster these relationships. When that happens, it may feel easier to devote themselves to work rather than find and build new relationships. But this is not a good long-term plan.

We each have different reasons for wanting to reclaim our lives and find time for ourselves. In your case, I hope you are doing this for *yourself*. If so, your challenge is to become clear about why you want to change things. Do you want to start a hobby, or have more time to spend with friends or family?

Working towards a goal is easier than moving away from a busy schedule. Nature abhors a vacuum and will fill your free time with random 'time wasters' if you don't identify ahead of time what you want to do with the extra time you make available. Please become clear about what you wish to do with the free time you create and that will be the goal you work towards.

Looking for some ideas to get you started on planning for the anticipated 'free' time? Here are some of the popular activities that other entrepreneurs have identified as desired goals:

Take better care of my health, to live longer.
Spend more time with my family.
Enrich my personal life (dating or time with friends).
Take up or reclaim a former hobby,
to do more things I enjoy.
Spend more time with the children in my life.
Enjoy child energy. Try playing a game or
following their lead.
Take a vacation!
Do something special with friends.
Attend my church, mosque, synagogue or temple.
Read or write more.
Travel more.
Rest awhile and see what happens.
Volunteer for a charity that I support.
To make a difference in the world.

When my big brother, my hero, died of a heart attack at age 50, I was hit by the realization of my own mortality. I made a list of the things I wanted to do before I turned 50. I understand that it's now called a 'bucket list'. Very few things on that list had to do with my business. There was a trip to Hawaii, starting this business, social activities with friends, climbing the CN Tower, writing my first book, *The Mentors Circle,* among other things. I wanted to leave a legacy. It took me 11 years to tick off everything on that bucket list. Luckily, I did not die at 50, but my life course was altered significantly. My brother's death made a huge difference in my life. The silver lining behind that loss was finding out what I wanted to do before it was too late. And today, I keep going. I'm much happier because of the reality jolt of that big loss. But you don't need to experience a great loss to turn your life around. You just need the desire to do so, and specific goals to aim towards. The goals will help you get organized and get more done.

You can't add years to your life, but you CAN add life to your years. If I live to be 80 years of age, I have a little over 8,000 days left. I want each of those days to be significant. How many days/years do you have before you turn 80?

50 more years = 18,250 days
40 more years = 14,600 days
30 more years = 10,950 days

Do you know what you want to achieve before you turn 80? You may want to create your own bucket list. Be specific. It will motivate you to free up the time for those dreams and goals.

The Lifestyle Audit and commitment to goals helps you understand your current situation. Another great exercise is to ask yourself the following questions:

Do I differentiate self-management from time management?
Between wants and needs?
Between what is urgent and what is important?

d) Differentiating self-management from time management.

It's important to differentiate self-management from time management. Time ticks along – you can't manage time. You can only manage your actions. Productive people usually have a pattern to their day. Through self-management you can get yourself ready, revitalized and focused to begin work. If you read something here that you have read before, but have never tried, try it on for size. Put an action plan in place to test a variety of new habits that help you get more done. Some habits will stick; others won't. Test and measure what works for you. Then do more of what works!

Six months ago, I decided that I wanted to meditate more often. I saw that I had a more focused day when I meditated. I had been practicing meditation sporadically and decided that I wanted to increase my practice to five times per week. It was bumpy at first. Each morning, I had to decide - should I meditate or not? Then, I explored the idea of meditating each and every day. I found that it's much easier to do something daily, than occasionally.

In general, new practices take 21-28 repetitions to settle into habits. Press on. Keep trying new ideas to find out if you can adopt them as your own new habits.

A classic example is deciding to exercise three times per week. It takes about 21 times for you to own this new habit, so you need to exercise three times a week for seven weeks! Press on. Build it into your schedule. Block off specific time in your planner. Bribe yourself. What would work as a bribe for you? A lunch out or time with a friend? Can you find a workout buddy to meet at a specific time? That is something that motivates me. By the time seven weeks are up, you will find yourself looking forward to your workouts and it will be hard to give up this new habit that makes your mind and body feel so good. By the way, if you establish a habit, but break that routine and want to get back to it, it will take fewer repetitions to reintegrate the habit into your life. You can recall how good it made you feel and work towards it.

Another self-management way that's worked for a few clients is to *tap into your superhero self.* What are the super powers you want to tap into? Do you think that The Flash gets the most done? Become The Flash when you want to get more done! Is Batman the most resourceful? Does Green Lantern have the most willpower? Take on your favourite superhero when you're worn out and want to push through to accomplish something on a Friday afternoon, so you can take some time off on the weekend.

Do you remember when you learned to drive? Your instructor taught you to look way ahead to monitor what was coming up on the road ahead in the way of congestion or construction. After you've been driving for a number of years, your view of what's in front can shrink back, so that you're only monitoring the brake lights of the car in front of you! When you've got your nose to the grindstone—preoccupied with immediate concerns, you can forget to take the long view.

Managing your time is scheduling your work and personal time in advance so you plan to function better. Your daily planner is an important tool to help you take the long view to get more done. Using your planner helps you:

* take a big-picture perspective of your entire week or month ahead
* prioritize your activities better
* plan your time in advance
* identify busy time frames

* block off time to work on specific projects
* plan the transit time from one appointment to another

Use your planner to focus on the practical day-to-day. When you separate the planning from the implementation of the actual jobs, you become more effective as you can then go from one job to the other on your list, without wasting time figuring out which job to do next, while juggling the multiple priorities of running a business.

Everyone notes appointments in their planner. But when you use this practical tool to block off time for specific projects, tasks, and ideas that are important to your life in general and not just to your business, you will make steady progress in each of these projects. Then, when urgent matters crop up to trump your plan, you are not distracted by them. You know that you have marked 'write report' in your planner for Friday afternoon and you remember how important that project is to you. You are aware of that deadline and you will follow through on it if nothing more urgent demands priority. Even if that happens, you know to reallocate the time to finish the scheduled project.

A great time management trick is setting false deadlines. These have often saved me. If a report is due at the end of the month, my goal will be to complete a draft by mid-month and work on edits for the remaining weeks. That way, if an urgent job arises, (which often happens) I can submit an updated draft. Depending on what priorities I'm juggling, a B+ report may be good enough. If it must be an A+ report, then I have to make time to improve the final draft and submit it when it's ready. Either way–having a draft ready two weeks early makes it easier to reach my deadlines. Being on time is easier to measure than the quality of the report and is sometimes more important to your clients or colleagues.

We can be judged as unreliable if we don't meet our deadlines, and this affects our credibility and reputation.

Aunt Betty's Story

My aunt Betty had an ingenious way of dealing with drop in guests. She lived in Nova Scotia and kept a hat strategically positioned on the foyer table. When someone rang the bell, she would pick up her hat to answer the door. If she wanted to see you, she would exclaim "I just got in the door, come on in." If she was not feeling like company, she would say "I'm just headed out the door. Can you call me later and we'll set up a time to get together?" It worked every time!

I have prompted many clients to use physical space and body language in their offices in a similar strategy to Aunt Betty's. If you work in a busy office and have an extra chair at your desk, it's an invitation for people to sit down to chat awhile. Move the chair away from your desk and move it back when you have appointments.

When someone overstays their drop-by visit, stand up when you're ready for the visit to end. If the person is not there on urgent business, 9 times out of 10 they will stand up too. Walk with them towards the door or exit and they will probably leave. If not, explain that you must get back to your work, as you're working to deadline on a project. (If you work in a cubicle or open-concept office, try posting a do-not-disturb sign or "Quiet, please. On voice conference" notice.)

The Aquarium Story

A time management guru enters the conference room, approaches a table at the front of the room that has an aquarium on it and some rocks beside it. She carefully places the rocks into the aquarium and asks the delegates if it is full. Participants point out that there are spaces in between the rocks. She takes a bucket of pebbles out from under the table and pours them in to fill the spaces. She asks again if it is full. A few people inform her that there are still some spaces in between the pebbles and rocks. She picks up a bag of sand beside the table and sprinkles it over the rocks and pebbles and it sifts down to fill in most of the spaces. Finally, everyone agrees that the aquarium is full. She then takes a large jug of water and pours it into the aquarium. The sand absorbs all the water.

Now, the point of this story is NOT that we can always fit something else in to an already 'full' container. Rather, it is that there is *only one way* to fit all these materials into that tight space. If she disassembles the rocks, pebbles, sand and water, she cannot fit them all in – in any other order. If she puts the sand or pebbles in first, there will be rocks left over. She must plan where to put the rocks first, and then the other materials fit in around them. *Plan your rocks first!*

What does that mean? The rocks are the solid pieces of work that need to be done first. If that aquarium is a visual representation of 24 hours or even a week of time, what jobs and blocks of time must we slot in to have a productive day/week? We must create time for those big chunks of work. The smaller jobs will work around these rocks. The interruptions (calls, e-mails, and people dropping by your office) will fit around your more important work, when you plan in advance and block off some time for those rocks.

If you want to complete your important work, plan your rocks (big/important jobs) and block off time in advance for them. The rest of the work will still get done, but around these main jobs. During your planning time, you can identify work that can be done by others or delete less important work that would be nice to get done but is not critical. You may even figure out how to delegate, dovetail or streamline some jobs to get more done in less time.

e) Templates Help you Plan

Creating templates to plan out your workweek can be very useful. Try developing a weekly template; test-drive it for one month and measure how effective it is for you. That will be enough time to find out if it improves your productivity.

Some of my clients find it handy to create a template for their week. Typically, the business template divides each day into blocks of time. Often, there is a morning block of 9-12, an afternoon block of 1-4 and the evening timeslot of 7-9 pm. You would place a "rock" into each block of time. This will help focus your efforts on one important task per block. For example, it's important to remember to make your sales calls early in the week (Tuesday is best) and it often works well to do your administration on Friday afternoon. It's important to realize, from the beginning that a template is meant to be a guide to help you block off your time. It's meant to be a guide and it's important not to feel too restricted by it. It's meant to support you, not distract you from your work.

The first step is to identify the 'rocks' in your business. To create your template or overall plan for a week, review the list below of tasks you may typically need to do every week. Please add any that are specific to your world.

Identify your Business Rocks *Personal Rocks*

Networking	Fitness
Sales calls	Personal maintenance
Prospecting meetings	Family time
Client time	Social dates
Admin. (billing, banking, filing)	Medical appointments
Research and development	Special Interests/Courses
Social media	Community involvement
New development	

List or add your categories here:

_____

_____

_____

_____

_____

_____

_____

_____

The 'pebbles' and the 'sand' will take care of the rest of the time you have around your 'rocks' or main tasks. The key things will get done first, and that's the secret to building your business. Once you plan the broad strokes, the details will get done. Remember, there's more to your life than your business. Include personal, family and social time.

Your template could look something like this:

	Monday	*Tuesday*	*Wednesday*	*Thursday*	*Friday*
	Planning day	Outreach	Client time	Client time	Future plans
Am	Catch up, planning/review	Social media	Networking, Appointments	Networking, Appointments	Prospecting, Meetings
Am	Research & development	Sales calls	Client time	Client time	Research & development
Pm	Delegating weekly work	Client time	Client time	Client time	Administrative work
Pm	New development				

You get to decide if your template of your planned workweek runs for 5 or 7 days. Review your "rocks" from the earlier exercise, so you can block off time for each of these important activities. Consider the activities that contribute to a successful week for both your business and personal life.

After you've built your own template, you might then designate offsite or outside-the-office days and onsite or 'inside' days. You'll list the work that falls into each of these categories and find out how many days you need for each. You'll find that jobs can easily dovetail when you plan an outside day for running the errands required in your business.

When you build a list of recurring outside jobs, it becomes easier to delegate. You can even hire someone for a day to run these errands. Each day of your workweek schedule has two to four blocks of activities. There might be two blocks in the a.m. and two blocks in the p.m. Each block of activity would be 2 or 3 hours.

For example, Monday could be designated as a 'Planning day,' with the a.m. dedicated to activities like planning and review, or research and development. The pm could be dedicated to activities such as delegating weekly work assignments and new business development.

Tuesday could be designated as an 'Outreach day'. The a.m. activities might include store visits and sales calls. Your p.m. activity could be dedicated to client time.

Your business template might look like this.

	Monday	*Tuesday*	*Wednesday*	*Thursday*	*Friday*
	Inside day	Outside day	Outside day	Outside day	Inside day
Am	Planning/ catch up/ review	Store visits (west end)	Appointments (east end)	Networking, Appointments	Prospecting, Meetings
Am	Sales phone calls	Client time	Client time	Client time	Research & development
Pm	Delegating weekly work	Client time	Client time	Client time	Administrative work
Pm					

This template will help you plan the broad strokes for a strong week. As you test this schedule for a few weeks, you will tweak it to incorporate information and business activities that may have been overlooked. Creating the template does not mean that you have to stick to it each and every week. Not at all. It means that you will work your schedule with the intention of covering all your identified 'rocks' to create a successful week.

When you plan time for friends and family on your work schedule template, this special time is more apt to happen.

The wonderful thing about owning your own business is that you can work as little or as much as you want. People are often drawn to self-employment to have this flexibility and then end up losing sight of that goal. They start to work harder, not smarter. So I ask you: do you want to work smarter or harder? I know my own answer.

It's easy to see working harder as a badge of honour. We were rewarded as children for working hard. There's an adrenaline hit that we get when we work hard and accomplish our goals. The more challenging, the bigger the rush. An adrenaline rush usually occurs when the body senses danger, the 'Fight or Flight" moment. Our heart rate increases, and pleasure-giving endorphins are released by the pituitary gland and our breathing rate ramps up. The result of all this extra oxygen, energy and hormones is the adrenaline high, and this euphoric feeling can last for hours. I think it's the last addiction to be seen in a positive light. It's not as healthy as you might think. As with any addiction, we need more of the substance over time. We need to look for bigger challenges to trigger our stress response. So, we work harder and overcommit ourselves to get that next rush of adrenaline.

Then, we got into the habit of working harder. We start to say things like "I work best under pressure". And suddenly, we start feeling tired or burned out. We just try to keep going, without assessing how we can change things. We start to accept that we need to work this hard. Others might say that we are workaholic or tell us that we work too hard.

The consequences are many: exhaustion, weight gain, intimacy problems. Workaholics are impatient. They want things done now, are quick to judge and make snap decisions that frequently lead to serious errors in judgment.

If change was easy, you wouldn't resist it. Change takes you out of your comfort zone. When you are clear on the overriding reasons why you want to change a habit, it helps motivate you to shift things. Ask yourself these questions.

What do you want to change?

1)_____

2)_____

3)_____

Why do you want this change?

1)_____

2)_____

3)_____

Who will you ask for support on this journey?

1)_____

2)_____

3)_____

It's time to make a conscious decision. You're a grown up! Working smarter can shift you from a workaholic to a *workafrolic!* How does that sound? Workafrolics can have fun while getting a lot of serious work done.

You CAN block Fridays off or take several micro-vacations and plan around them. You can do what works best for you and still meet your family and financial commitments. And, surprisingly enough, once you are committed to taking time off and focusing on how to build and run your business within assigned timeframes, you can become efficient. You work towards that new deadline, and "git 'er done," to get out of the office.

I hope these tips for distinguishing between self-management and time-management were useful to you.

DID YOU KNOW?

Did you know that if you block off time at the beginning of the year for your vacations, they are more likely to happen? Your schedule can accommodate your plans. Of course, there may be a situation where you need to shift that block of vacation time for a special client or to accommodate a deadline, but make sure you only do so for very important work for which payment is guaranteed, and you choose another suitable time for your holiday

When you plan a holiday with significant others, you must stay the course and honour your time off with them. Brainstorm this commitment with your support team to find a suitable solution. Remember which relationships are most important to your life and act accordingly.

Your family may start to feel that they are no longer important to you. Whereas your clients see how important they are to you all year long, so they may be understanding about your need for a break from your work. You may have to remind them that you are an awesome business owner as well as a human being who needs a break.

I take an hour on Sunday evenings to plan my week-at-a-glance and then text or e-mail a few friends to plan a lunch as my reward. It's delightful to plan the time in advance to ensure that happens. When I leave it to chance, it's less likely to happen.

f) *Needs vs Wants*

How do you distinguish between Needs vs Wants? Needs are must-do activities. And wants are nice-to-do activities. Do you know the difference?

- You need money to pay your monthly bills and plan for your future.
- You want money to pay for indulgences and to expand your business.
- You need shelter and food.
- You want to own a luxury home and have lavish meals.
- You need to take breaks to recharge your energy and passion for your work.
- You want to be the energizer bunny, who works longer than anyone else.

Or did I get that last one mixed up? Working hard on your business is great, but you need breaks to recharge and keep your life in balance.

These examples are exaggerated, of course, to make a point. You decide what you need to have and what you want to have. There's an advantage to planning in advance, in that you can budget time and money for your plans. There are fewer surprises when you identify what you want and need and plan accordingly. Just remember that time is your most limited resource. Spend it wisely. You can never recoup lost time, but you CAN recoup lost dollars.

g) Urgent vs Important

Urgent tasks rear their ugly heads and must be dealt with. These are deadline-driven activities (e.g., project launches, special events, payroll, publication deadlines, tax filings).

Important tasks wait in the shadows for you to notice them. These activities must be done to keep your business going (e.g., prospecting, marketing, business planning). Once you differentiate what is urgent from what is important, you can decide how to get it all done. Every week presents a mix of urgent and important tasks that you need to do. If you only deal with the urgent tasks, you will burn out, and your business is likely to suffer.

As a business owner, you must remember to add some of your important personal tasks (e.g., maintaining your primary relationships, health and home). Add time for these into your plan. This will keep you healthy and happy in business and personal time.

Are you getting things done in a timely manner? You may need to learn to prospect, plan or sell more effectively. Whatever it is that you need to learn, you benefit when you find a way to learn it quickly. Time is limited, and doing things effectively and efficiently is key to being successful in business. Who has time to personally learn all the things we need to learn? You can reduce your learning curve by reading books, doing online research, and consulting with mentors.

What can you **delete, delegate, or dovetail** to get more done, more efficiently and more effectively? After you've made your plan, how can you implement it?

Creating action plans are as important as planning the work. Who is going to do the various tasks and when?

One last important question in understanding yourself and your style of doing business is your answer to the question 'Do I recognize the importance of letting go?'

h) *Letting go*

You must accept that there are only so many activities that can be done. Go through your list first and put brackets around the things you can let go of doing. Then, ask yourself: Who else can do them? Or indeed, must they really be done?

Once you decide which activities you can let go, you can review the 'want to get done' activities in a new light.

I have a few clients who pull all-nighters on a regular basis to catch up or get it all done. When I begin to discuss this situation with them, they get defensive and tell me that it doesn't happen all that often. I disagree. Working all night long is not an acceptable way for a business to run. These business owners are often single by choice, or are with partners who are very tolerant. They fill their time with 'want to get done' activities. There's no time left to spend unstructured time in getting to know someone better. There's no time for a relationship.

Ask yourself these few questions:

How important is that activity to my bottom line?
Why do I want to do this activity?
What will happen if I don't do it?
Who else could do this activity for me?
Is there a quiet time (seasonally or weekly) that I could plan to do this activity?

Story 1: Letting go

Like many clients, when Joanna tried to handle her own social media, she got distracted and spent more time than she intended to on Facebook posts or monitoring Twitter feeds. She has found that delegating the bulk of that work saves her time. Of course, she writes some of the content, but has other people write the rest and delegates all of the posting of that content.

When Joanna tested and measured the impact of delegating this work, she found it had little impact on her results.

Story 2: All in good time

Almost four years ago, I decided not to write this book. I felt that it would take too much time and it was not all that high on my list of priorities. Yet, the book project kept coming up on my 'want to do' list. I started to realize how much I wanted to write this book. I wanted to reach out to more people who need this information, people who I could not possibly meet face to face through my business, Office Mentors. I began to think of how I could delegate other 'work' in order to carve out time to write.

I also built in the support I needed to write as effectively as possible. I signed up for a writing retreat and treated it as a break from the day-to-day. And I joined an online writing course that gave me a strict Sunday deadline to submit new work for constructive feedback. I met most of those deadlines. Then I booked a summer holiday with family where I could write in a relaxed manner while they were out at work. It was a satisfying and rewarding experience.

I asked a few readers, business owners and editors to give me feedback on the information in this book, so I could make it even more useful to you. Everything has its time. You can get to the important things right after the urgent ones are dealt with, and you can let the others go. It does not mean that they will never get done.

> *"The bad news is that time flies. The good news is that you're the pilot."*
>
> Michael Altshuler
> *American speaker, authority on*
> *value-centered living and competitive edge selling.*

CHAPTER 2

Creating Your Own Recipe or Your Recovery Plan

---

a. Time Management vs Self-Management
b. Clarify Your Values
c. Technology
d. The 3 Ds: *Delegate, Dovetail, Delete*

Chapter 2
Creating Your Own Recipe or Your Recovery Plan

a) Time Management vs Self-Management

Become more aware of how you procrastinate. We all do it. The first step in awareness is to recognize that you do procrastinate. Next, figure out what you do when you're procrastinating. This helps you catch yourself, and re-direct your energy.

Start by looking at some real examples shared by clients:

- Craig wants to work on a project, and gets distracted by online research that takes up most of his day.
- Preet tidies up her piles of paperwork and makes her office look nice, instead of reading resumes.
- When Jack considers what to make for dinner, he spends an hour reading recipes!
- Brian plans a lunch break with a friend and ends up going shopping on his way back.
- Sam checks his e-mail, Facebook, and LinkedIn too often.
- Susan starts to listen to TED talks and finds it tough to pull herself away and get back to work.
- Paul walks the dog and that ends up 'kidnapping' his day.
- Nadia spends all night researching a new project online.
- While eating lunch, Lucy watches a TV show that lulls her into naptime. She wakes up with a start, realizing she's lost track of the time.

Next, look within using this four-step process:

1. Ask yourself, are you doing what needs to get done today?
2. Identify what you do when you're avoiding doing what needs to get done.
3. Bring awareness to your actions. Catch yourself in the act when you start to procrastinate.
4. Make a decision to get back on track.

To make this easier on yourself, try to ease into the moment. For example, make a deal with yourself: get that job done, and then go for a short walk or have a piece of chocolate. I've been writing for a couple of hours now, but I'll quit to have my treat soon. Promise! And when I feel as if I need a break, I'll set my "happy apple timer" for 15 minutes and allow myself to do something else. The ringing of my timer helps me get back on track.

Another procrastination buster is to just jump in and start the job you dread. Getting started is half the battle, right? When a job overwhelms you, it's important to chunk it down into manageable pieces of work. Start at the beginning, with one small step. Most jobs become manageable as you get into the nuts and bolts of them. If you need to get it done but can't seem to get going, identify what you need in the way of support. Reach out and set up a three-hour motivational call to work on those frog jobs. You know, those yucky jobs that you naturally avoid doing.

b) *Clarify Your Values*

What are your personal values around people? Which relationships do you value the most? Arrange this list in your order of priority, from 1 to 7, with one being your top priority.

Parents, Siblings, Children, Friends, Yourself, Life Partner, Business Contacts.

1) _____

2) _____

3) _____

4) _____

5) _____

6) _____

7) _____

Do you create enough time for the top three people on this list? You may have listed someone in the top three who you know is important to you, yet do you show them how they are valued? Do they feel that they are really among your top people to spend time with?

Next, clarify your personal values around other things in your life. Arrange this list in priority order for yourself, 1 being the highest priority to 9 being the lowest priority.

Business, Home, Entertainment, Health, Vacation, TV, Sleep, Food, Learning.

1) _____

2) _____

3) _____

4) _____

5) _____

6) _____

7) _____

8) _____

9) _____

Do you make enough time for the important things on this list? What do you want to do more often? If you could have 25 hours tomorrow, what would you do with the extra hour? Make more time for that activity now.

When you have time leftover, you can fill it with something consciously or make the unconscious choice to work more. Make no mistake, even your unconscious choice is a choice.

If you want to make another choice, create a plan to do that. If you want to help your life partner understand how important they are to you, consider what they might like or enjoy. Everyone's different. Buy them a small gift on the way home, or get home early enough to make a favorite dinner, or turn off the cell phone, sit down and listen to their day, offer to give them a massage, write out a special card to tell them exactly how much you appreciate what they do, or carve out time to take them on a mystery date. If you choose to do a few of these things, they would feel how much they mean to you.

c) Technology

Some say I have bad computer karma. I push a button on my computer and it doesn't work. You can come into my office and push the same button, and it does what it's supposed to do. That's why I need more computer support than other people. I accept this graciously. I also realize that I'm an internet immigrant, rather than a native. Anyone born after 1990 is considered a native in the computer world. I gather new information each day. I make slower progress than the generation who grew up using computers. I take notes when someone teaches me something new and I use those notes.

Technology changes. New programs are designed every day that can support your work. Do you spend time trying them out? Then you're an early adopter.

If you get a kick out of having the newest technology, and it's not taking away time from your business, keep at it. If you don't need to be up-to-date on high tech, slow down a bit. It takes a lot of time away from your business to stay informed (research) in order to be an early adopter. The latest tech is often plagued with start-up bugs that are time wasters in themselves.

Here's a tip about managing technology in your day-to-day that has helped many entrepreneurs. Before leaving the office, leave an old fashioned paper note on your computer with the first thing you need to get done when you start your next work day. It's best if you pick a yucky 'frog' job. When you begin work, you'll be tempted to check your e-mails first thing. But do that first job, first. Your e-mails are filled with other people's priorities, and they take you away from your own important work.

Take a digital detox now and again. Voluntarily withdraw from technology to fully realize how dependent you've become on your various electronic devices. Once, I was given notice that my office would be without power for a whole day the following week. I began to make plans to work elsewhere, when I stopped to consider other options. Then instead, I set up an out-of-office notice on my e-mail and voice mail. I called my father and we spent a wonderful day together. I consciously chose to spend quality time with someone who is important to me.

Check out the short video on the officementors.com site to learn more about the benefits of taking a digital detox.

d) The 3 Ds: Delegating, Dovetailing, Deleting

When you find you have too much to do, it's time to take a step back and look at the larger picture of your work situation. You might be able to find someone to delegate some tasks to, or group some tasks together in order to dovetail work, or reprioritize less important tasks or delete them off your to-do list altogether.

Do you prefer to make sales calls or do you like some other aspect of your work? Do you procrastinate over doing your paperwork, invoicing or bookkeeping? What jobs do you like best or least in your business?

To prepare for your work plan makeover, keep a running list of all the jobs that you do in a typical week. Then rate them according to your enjoyment level, on a scale of 1 to 10 from least to most enjoyable. Once you've ranked these activities, you can create a plan to delegate, dovetail or delete the lower-scoring jobs.

My typical jobs each week   *Rate 1-10 for Enjoyment Levels*

_____   _____

_____   _____

_____   _____

Which jobs on this list do you consistently procrastinate around? Put a letter 'F' (for Frog) beside those jobs. We'll come back to these yucky, slimy frog jobs soon.

Once you've scored your jobs, make a new list of the activities that you rated below five. Now, take time to brainstorm with a mentor or peer to imagine how to get those jobs off your work plan. If you spend an hour figuring out how to delegate those activities, it will pay off in the long run.

Jobs ranking low in enjoyment   (1-5)

_____

_____

_____

_____

Delegating

Which jobs can be delegated? If you think you have no one to delegate to, I ask you to take a moment to think outside the box to find no-cost or low-cost support for your business.

Some business owners save time by delegating their deliveries to a courier service. A reliable courier service can handle some of your regular trips, saving you time, while eliminating frustration. One photographer arranged to have her printed proofs delivered twice a week at minimal cost, which saved her time and offset travel costs. A medical clinic had their clinic's urine and blood tests delivered by special courier to the laboratory for testing, delegating a task that no-one wanted to do at the end of a busy day.

Many business owners delegate their bookkeeping and when they crunch the numbers, actually save money at the end of the year! When you put systems in place and have work completed by a professional, you can write off all the expenses incurred on outsourcing and at the same time ensure all relevant details are included and accurate. This can save you time and money.

An *operations manual* is a great way to detail routine jobs that can be assigned to others. If you have part-time or fulltime contractors, volunteers, co-op students, interns or regular staff, an operations manual or electronic document can save you lots of time when assigning or delegating work. Creating an operations manual is an important task that is not urgent, until you need it. When a key person leaves, even for a holiday, it's useful to be able to easily delegate their responsibilities.

Creating such a manual is not a difficult task. It's as simple as opening a document and saving it as your 'Operations Manual.' The next time you explain to a helper how to do a task, ask that person to keep notes and type up the instructions in a document. Review it to ensure that all the steps are there, and it will be ready to 'direct' the next person. There will be minimum training time required the next time you delegate. Ask the new person to read the instructions, try the task first, and then ask if they have questions. Treat this draft manual as a living document, and adjust it as needed. Co-op students and part-time staff have typed up my entire Operations Manual. This makes delegating much easier!

For student co-op help, contact a local high school, as most schools have a co-op or mentor program. This program can place a student who is interested in a specific industry to gain experience, for a school term. The students get a school credit for learning about your business while working for you. Placements offer the student an understanding of what is involved in being part of a workplace setting. Discuss your needs with the teacher in charge of that program. This option works well when you need someone to staff a storefront, answer phones, support social media plans, or do online research. A recent co-op student created awesome videos for my web site. Communication is the key to finding out what a student is already skilled at or wants to learn. These students can help you update your current skill set. Even when they don't know how to accomplish something, you can ask them to do the preliminary research to find out how to accomplish it.

Large cities have English-as-a-Second-Language schools or programs. Speak to the principal or director of the school to find out if volunteer placement is a part of their program. If not, they may still be willing to post a description of the volunteer position to find a student suitable for your company. This can be a particularly good match for technical or computer work (e.g., SEO or online marketing plan). Is there a government agency that works with new immigrants near you? Agencies in many cities find volunteer placements for immigrants to gain valuable work experience in their country of choice. Once they work on a project, you may want to train them to take care of certain tasks on a weekly basis. This gives them a better chance of finding a job in their industry of choice. There may even be a program that subsidizes their wage for a specified time as there is a reasonable expectation that the training you provide will lead to a job.

Church, mosque, temple or synagogue bulletins are also a great place to request a volunteer for a specific project. There may be an executive in transition or a retired person in the community who would enjoy taking on an interesting or challenging project. In addition, you can explore online searches to find barter or exchange services that might be useful to your particular needs. Craigslist and Kijiji both have sections that may help you find the right exchange of services.

College or university placements take a little more effort to obtain and maintain. You need to meet with the institution's program supervisor and provide progress reports on students' progress. The benefit is that these more experienced students can help with advanced level work. Your company may need a draftsperson or a new designer. Find the specific program at that school that trains students in the field in which you require support and discuss what you need and what's possible. Many of these student placements are so successful that the new graduates end up being hired by the companies the following summer, or fulltime upon graduation.

Another route to consider is hiring a *virtual assistant* (VA). There's a large pool of VAs willing to do work from their own offices via the internet. They can do any work you require from website updates, social media promotion, bookkeeping and billing, to booking your appointments or your travel arrangements, etc. They can be working in another city, province or even country. You may end up hiring two of them to meet different needs. I urge you to consider which of these ideas suits your business best and build in the support you require.

A more traditional route would be to hire a staff person or subcontractor to help you on a regular or irregular basis in your own office. This works well for some business owners. They advertise locally and find someone who lives nearby. Try posting an ad in a local on-line paper or Facebook community page. You can even put up a flyer in neighborhood stores. Local is often a perfect fit.

Building in the support you need frees up time to think clearly and do the higher-level work that earns your business more money. That pays for the support you require and allows you to take time away from your business to recharge yourself.

If you're working in a one-person office and those 'frog' jobs keep gathering, here is another tip that may work for you. I have two skilled administrative support people who I bring into my office on an as-needed basis to catch up on certain tasks. I bring them in one at a time to tackle the backlog list of jobs that I've been putting off so I can focus on the work that only I can complete. If the list is particularly long, we tackle it together.

Dovetailing

Next, consider which of your activities can be dovetailed. These jobs that can be done simultaneously or concurrently by yourself or someone else. You may rate some jobs 'below five' because they are just plain boring! A computer programmer I worked with taught himself to juggle while monitoring his pilot programs. He had to keep one eye on the screen, and that was perfect for learning to juggle. Other activities, like filing, can be made more enjoyable by listening to a lecture or business book. A few speakers I've mentored send their handouts to the copy shop via e-mail, and then ask a support person to pick them up while they are out running errands. Or, they pick them up themselves while they are out buying office supplies. Any office can be run more efficiently if a list of errands is maintained. When someone is about to leave the office, they could scan the list to see if any of those errands are along their route.

Deleting

Ask yourself what activities can be deleted off your to-do list. There are some jobs that don't need to be done any more. This requires a fresh look at your modus operandi. When a system changes through technology advancements, some people continue doing the same old thing the same old way. For example, you don't need to save old business cards, once they've been entered into your database. Or, you could start using LinkedIn to track your contacts, who usually update their details when they move or change jobs. It makes it much easier to stay in touch.

Redundant supplies can be cleared out once newer versions come into your office, which also creates storage space and reduces visual clutter.

Of course, some jobs can only be done by you, in which case you're stuck with them. Set deadlines for each task, and consider how you can reward yourself for getting them done on time. For example, block off time to edit a report just before you meet a friend for lunch. This gives you a deadline and offers some motivation with the reward of lunch with a friend.

You can add time to your day and income to your business by delegating, dovetailing, and deleting your lower-rated activities (see list above). You may add years to your life by doing more of what you love to do!

"A journey of a thousand miles begins with a single step."

Lao Tzu
Chinese Philosopher

CHAPTER 3

Be the Head Chef Or Getting and Staying Organized

    a. Organizing your Physical Space
    b. How to Start
    c. Daily, Weekly, Monthly
    d. Goal Charts
    e. Accountability
    f. Motivational Focus Program
    g. Personal vs Business

Chapter 3
Be the Head Chef or Getting and Staying Organized

a) Organizing your Physical Space

Long ago, I read of a time study, which revealed that we lose up to an hour per day looking for lost papers. I can vouch for the truth in this study, especially since I usually juggle several projects at the same time, generating a ton of paperwork. My desk often ends up looking like a paperwork pan lasagna! On good days, I keep only a few piles on my desk and I know exactly what is in each one of them. Each pile represents an 'active' project. On top of each pile, there is a hand written paper with a list of the steps to be taken to complete that project.

Clients call me in when they are ready to learn about other organizing options and develop new habits at work. We discuss their needs and possible solutions. There is no one-size-fits-all answer. I've set clients up with files, binders, and even baskets to store their papers. There is a solution to suit your working style. Keep searching, test and measure to find out what works for you, personally.

Remember the Sesame Street game of 'which one of these things doesn't belong? From a young age, we are taught to sort objects.

When you're feeling overwhelmed, it's helpful to sort through the stuff on top of your desk. Clients tell me that they feel at peace once they prioritize their projects and know where everything is kept. They feel a sense of being in control and security. It puts their minds at ease.

b) How to begin?

Sit in front of your desk and demote or move anything that's two feet in front of your body. If you sit down with your hands together and your elbows out along the edge of the desk, is there space for you to work? Think in terms of training yourself to keep this space clear so that you can easily work on an active project. Consider this your 'active space.' Do not let papers or computers move in here. Tape a 'NO Loitering Allowed' sign if you must. This space is for the 'project of the hour.' If you sit in front of a desktop computer full time, set up a secondary workspace for active projects. If you have a laptop computer in front of you, clear a space to move it out of your 'active space' when you're ready to work on a project. I installed a keyboard tray to house a full sized keyboard that I plug into my laptop computer when I'm working. When I'm not working, I can shift the laptop away from my active workspace.

Once you have delineated your 'active space,' the next step is to identify which office items you use on a daily basis. Some examples might be your;

Computer
Phone
Stapler
Tape
Pens

These necessities will remain on your desk. The other items are often called delayed decisions, and they create messy build up. You don't know where to put them, but they have to be dealt with eventually to avoid clutter, and bring some peace of mind.

First of all;

> 1 Begin by removing everything from your desk surface.
> 2 Dust and clean your desk surface.
> 3 Create a list of the jobs that were on your desk.
> 4 Set up a file structure that you can use to store these papers, and retrieve them when you're ready to work on these projects.

What does this story mean to you? How might your office space be reorganized?

Consider these steps in reorganizing your office space:

1) Remove any broken or obsolete equipment. Make a list of what equipment you require in your office. Make a shopping list of things you need to purchase.

2) Remove any unnecessary items that have found their way into your office. Set a timer to race the clock or put on some favorite music before you begin. Work for a set amount of time to remove anything that does not belong in your office. You may want to set aside a box for items that are to be discarded.

3) Go through your bookshelves and purge the books you've read or don't need. Set up a shelf for extra books.

4) Purge any storage space or closets of clutter to free up room for storing other things. When you pack these items into boxes to go back into storage spaces, create a list of what's in the boxes and tape the list to the outside of the box. You can also keep that list in a binder or on your

computer, so you know what you have, if you need to retrieve items later.

5) Create categories for the leftover materials. Is there one main work focus for this office, or will you require a few different work zones?

6) Is it time to cull the files in your filing cabinet? This task is best done each year to avoid clutter and create storage space. I like to use different coloured file folders to specify the broad categories (e.g. green files for administration, blue for clients, yellow for special projects). If I were in your office, I would suggest adding an 'Action' section in the file cabinet closest to your work area. This can change your habit of keeping files on your desk. When you arrive at work, you open your file drawer, and have those files at your fingertips.

7) Put away anything that's drifted back onto your desk so you can maintain a clear place for you to work.

8) Remove anything that you don't use daily off your desk top. Put it on a nearby shelf. Decide if you typically use those items weekly or monthly. If weekly, keep on nearby shelves. If monthly, store it farther away or behind closed doors.

9) Work on developing the habit of stopping work 10-15 minutes before you leave the office to clear your desk and any other messy build up.

10) Block off time in your schedule to maintain your office. Depending on your working style, you may designate time on a weekly, monthly or quarterly basis. If you leave it to

do on an annual basis, the job becomes too large and daunting.

11) After a while, clutter tends to creep back into your office. Block off time in your schedule to clean up yourself, or bring in some support to help you get on top of it.

c) Daily, Weekly, Monthly Organization

Does it make sense to you to plan your work from the top down or the bottom up? Does a daily plan or a monthly plan appeal most to your style or nature of your work?

You're the boss. You get to set monthly goals first or the daily goals.

Many business owners who are overwhelmed cope best with a daily goals focus. They spend time fighting fires of everyday issues and can only see the 'crises de jour.'

When you set annual goals, you can break them down into quarterly and then monthly goals. Once you set monthly goals, you have a chance to break those down into weekly projects. Once you know what you want to accomplish each week, then you can estimate how much time it will take and block off some time in advance to make it happen.

For example, what if you decide to build your profile on the internet using social media. You would slot this goal into a specific month.

If you book yourself a spot in a seminar on social media, block off time before the seminar to learn what you can on the topic. Experience has shown that to get the most out of any seminar, you need to learn a few things before you attend. You can understand and integrate more of a new topic, when you have already learned a bit about the topic. The seminar date gives you a reason to learn more now. It takes an important task and makes it a more pressing task. Go off to the seminar with some informed questions.

After the seminar, follow up on what your learned by developing some SMART Goals (Specific, Measurable, Actionable, and Realistic, with a Timeline). If you decide to devote 5 hours per week learning more about social media, how to use LinkedIn or Facebook, and begin writing your blog, then you might want to create a plan to do so. The old adage "When we fail to plan, we plan to fail" rings true here.

It's tough to sit in front of a computer for long periods of time, so break the goal of 5 hours per week (on social media updates) into blocks of time throughout the week. For an hour per day, focus on learning or doing more to build your online business profiles, asking people you know about their approach to social media. Decide which hour in the workweek works best for you, and the people helping you, and block off that hour.

I understand my working style well enough to know that this hour must be during the morning, when I'm fresh and work at my best. I will resist doing something new and outside my comfort zone. I'll get busy doing the urgent jobs and that will squeeze out my important work. I book the hour each morning into my planner. I would block off a recurring 'appointment' at 8:30 each morning to work on my computer on learning (and doing) more around building my profile using social media.

Too many people take class after class and don't actually get to the 'doing' part of the learning process. The challenge is to implement the ideas that piqued your interest in the topic of study. The social media landscape changes so rapidly that we'll never gather all the information we need to get it 'right.' It's important to know how much or how little is 'enough' for you and make your social media updates on a schedule:

Monthly
Weekly
Daily

It would be equally valid to decide to spend an hour per day learning about social media and not attend a class at all; see where it goes. I know that approach does not suit my working style. I would end up letting other things get in the way, and put that important goal aside to work on other stuff.

Consider your own working style and which approach works best for you.

Remember, each day offers you a chance to have a fresh start. We have been conditioned to start fresh in January (the New Year) and September (the academic new year). Yet, truth be told, you can begin fresh any day. Try it. Create your plan and begin today. After all, it's the first day of the rest of your life!

Client Story

A client in the entertainment industry earned his income through using several of his talents. He was a professional artist and musician and had set up a graphic design company that did work for television studios. He had top of the line recording equipment and recorded music for other musicians as well. At our first appointment, we discussed his needs and wants, and I could see that he was doing all his work in the same work space. This created unnecessary work whenever he changed his focus and had to shift gears to a different job. This working style often led to chaos.

We started his reorganization plan by moving his desk in front of the window to improve his view. Then we developed zones to 'house' each of his diverse interests. We moved furniture around to establish a studio space, used a colourful carpet to define the space, and hung some of his larger artwork. He planned to purchase some other area rugs to hold the zones or work spaces that we had defined for other 'jobs.' Each zone looked beautiful and self contained, and he told me recently that the areas remain uncluttered.

Once we cleared his 'messy build-up' of clutter, we discussed a workable plan for him to spend 4 hours per week on maintaining this streamlined office. He is the boss, and he decides each week if he will work on it an hour per day, or all at once. He told me recently that he is developing new habits to maintain his office in less time each week. This was music to my ears. New habits make a big difference!

d) Goal Charts

Once you have a specific goal, how do you organize that big piece of work? It may appear too big to take on and have fuzzy edges like a daunting monster of a task. One client talks about "slaying" goals, and it works well for her. Use that metaphor if it speaks to you.

A goal chart can help you break any challenge down into chunks of work, and create the action steps that could become the focus of your implementation plan. When you capture your future work in a goal chart, it appears more manageable. You can focus on the one chunk of work that's next, rather than be overwhelmed by the prospect of the bigger goal.

This useful tool can help you clarify the steps needed in the next few weeks. Make your goals specific, actionable, measureable, realistic, and with a timeline. Those are SMART Goals. Please remember to reward yourself!

Hang that chart near your desk. Review it each morning to remind yourself which goals are important to you. You will get more done when you work away at your important goals. Sure--some of your monthly goals might get carried over into the next month. Yet, more of them will be accomplished when you use a monthly goal chart that is visible to you when you work.

OFFICE MENTORS – GOAL CHART

Your name _____

Date _____

Specific Goals	Step 1	Step 2	Step 3	Step 4	Step 5

This useful tool can help you clarify the steps needed in the next few weeks. Good luck! Make your goals specific, measurable and realistic, and remember to reward yourself! Utilize the WIN (What's Important Now) Principle.

"The path is clear, so why do you continue to throw stones before you?"
Chinese Proverb

e) Accountability

When you run into challenges with a particular goal, it's important to figure out what is getting in your way and assess what support you need to break through any blocks or barriers to your progress.

When the work is not going as planned, it's time to come up with a Plan B, or even a Plan C. Ask yourself, what would tempt me to complete this goal? Schedule some small indulgence and then consider that to be your reward for achieving the goal (a movie, a ballgame, a night out, a visit to an indoor garden, lunch with a friend). This reward can even act as a deadline to completing your goal.

If you're like many people, you might be more inclined to finish up a task if you ask someone else to follow up with you. This buddy system can be a great help. Even if you're a solopreneur, you can build an element of accountability with another person into your new plan.

With regard to this buddy system, I have a 'secret weapon,' called the **Motivational Focus Program (MFP) that really works for me and many other businesses.** When it's time to get those difficult jobs done, ask around to find someone who is grappling with a few of their own difficult jobs. It does not have to be the same type of work. Right now, I'm working on this book, and my friend is working on de-cluttering her home.

Invite your 'accountability buddy' to block off three hours of time and both of you promise to hold each other accountable for getting those yucky jobs done! Set up a time, say working together from 9am 'til noon, and get to it!

f) Motivational Focus Program

- 9am—Speak by phone or Skype for 2 to 3 minutes each to share what you plan to do over the next hour
- 10am—Touch base for another 2-3 minutes only. Each one of you share what happened. Did you stay on track? Did you get interrupted? Did you leave your project to do something else? Learn from your experience. Hold each other accountable. Use caring pressure, with humour. Celebrate any successes. Try again.
- 11am—Check in to share what happened and re-commit to a specific project for an hour.
- 12pm—Call to wrap up. Recap what was within your control and what was outside your control. What will you do differently next time?

This MFP program is so effective that I offer it as a fee for service. People learn a lot about their working style and get more done. Describe it to a friend or business associate and try it out. Choose someone you won't want to let down and you'll work extra hard to plow through your 'frog' projects!

Remember to reach out to others when you have a project that you don't know how to accomplish. If you have read *The Mentors Circle*, you may have heard of or already created your One Hundred Mentors form.

When I set a goal that's outside my knowledge base, I review my One Hundred Mentors form to decide who to call first. That person may not have the answer, but they may offer up an idea that will lead me to another person. I will gather the information I need to find out how to approach my new project. You can, too! From nuts to bolts, you can find out how it all fits together, and cut your learning curve by reaching out and talking to other people. If it feels like it would be too much trouble to create that form now, review your LinkedIn contacts to see if there is someone you know who has expertise in the area of your new project. Reach out to them to find out what you can learn.

g) *Personal vs Business*

There's often a tug of war between your personal and business lives or a teeter totter effect when one of your 'lives' is up on one side, and the other is down or vice versa. When you are focused on your business, your family and friends are waiting, somewhat neglected, on the other side. If we leave them alone too long, they will get up and leave to find other things to do. That can play havoc with your balancing act and cause you to come crashing down. Think about it. If you lose your business, you will lose your livelihood; if you lose your family or friends, you can find yourself married to your business. Which is more important to you? It's tough to choose, so you teeter back and forth between the two.

Running your own business can feel like feeding a time-sucking monster. Remember that you are the boss! You can leave in the middle of the day and go do something personal. You can come in late or leave work early. You are the boss who gets to decide how much you will feed your business. You need to learn to work smarter, not harder.

When my children were young, I worked from a busy home office. There were a few staff who also used my office as their work base. Yet, I stopped work every day to have an after-school snack with my children. I loved to hear about their day during those tea breaks. It's important to be honest with yourself. Do you want to have more time with your family and friends? How can you make that happen? Be creative in your approach.

"We cannot do everything at once, but we can do something at once."

Calvin Coolidge
US President (1923-1929)

CHAPTER 4

A Menu Makeover for a Better Life or Completing Present Projects

    a. List All Your Projects
    b. Blocking Off Time
    c. Rewarding Yourself

Chapter 4
A Menu Makeover for a Better Life or Completing Present Projects

a) List All Your Projects

Yes–it's a daunting concept. But well worth it for the clarify it brings. Take two pads of paper. Write 'Personal' on the first page of one of them, and 'Business' on the other. Or, open a document on your computer to begin your list. Have two headings: 'Personal' and 'Business.'

Now write out all your projects. No need to break the projects down into the tasks at this point. Just list the projects, in no particular order.

For example:

Personal

Get an oil change
Shop for baby shower
Paint front porch
Plant the garden
Clean the garage
Plan a holiday
Create scrapbook of last holiday
Begin working out at the gym
Take day off with Mom/Dad

Business

Clean up desk
Update website
Purge office files
Update business plan
Develop social media presence
Strengthen marketing plan
Get design done
Follow up on tradeshow leads
Write outline of book

Once you feel you have listed all the projects, it is quite normal to start feeling overwhelmed. It's tough to see in black and white just how much is on your to-do list. Those tasks and projects were there all along. This list just keeps them visible. I hang my lists on flip chart paper in my office and home and check them off as I accomplish each job. This helps me stay on track. Some clients prefer to keep them on their computer or on paper in a binder.

Both your business and personal lists will include things you must do, things you would like to do, and things that you don't really want to do, but feel obligated to do. Right?

So, categorize them accordingly and then focus on shortening the lists using the Delegating, Deleting and Dovetailing techniques you learned earlier.

Do you live with others? Maybe you can share some of your personal to-dos with a family member, roommate or friend. For example, I invited a friend who was out of work to help me paint the porch. We spent a wonderful afternoon painting and chatting. While he resisted the gift of money I offered, it was a fraction of the cost of hiring a professional.

Delegating in action

You can delegate tasks from your business list to staff, volunteers, interns or co-op students with planned check-in points. Another option is to hire a high school or college student weekly. You need to block off time to get this person started and check in regularly, but then they can do a fair bit of work on their own.

Check in at specific time intervals or when they have completed key steps. This is key to successful delegating.

Does your business have slow periods? I've asked co-op students working in my business to review my personal 'to do' list for anything they would like to get involved with for the experience.

One student, for example, who lived in an apartment wanted to know more about gardens. I asked her to bring gardening clothes the next day and bought my plants that evening.

In 15 minutes, I was able to teach her how to plant and went back to work in my home office, leaving the pots near their respective flower beds. I checked in with her on regular breaks and she enjoyed an afternoon in the garden with her own music. Later on, when I taught her about weeding, she was able to maintain the garden and enjoyed watching it thrive. For the rest of the summer, we ate lunch in 'our' garden whenever we had time.

This diversion from regular business work was a welcome break, and may have opened up a new door of possibility in her life.

Dovetailing in action

You can get more done when you leverage your energy by sharing larger projects.

You can also ask another person to assist you in a major purging project, as there are lots of decisions to make, as well as all the lifting and carrying.

Are some routine must-do tasks too confidential or complex to share? Capitalize on the time by using a voice-activated recorder to capture ideas or insights while purging or reviewing files.

You can also lighten any task by listening to great tunes, a recorded book or even a motivational podcast.

Podcasts allow you to listen to radio shows that you want, when you want. Why listen to a repeat of the news when you're doing another routine task, when you can listen to a program you enjoy or that expands your mind?

Deleting in action

Letting go of some things makes room for something more important. It's rather like finishing a book that bores you. Why bother? Life's too short. Choose projects and books wisely.

One project that lingered on my personal to-do list was finishing a soapstone sculpture I began years ago during an evening course. I had completed a few sculptures and loved this particular mother and child study. Still, I could never 'find the time' to complete it.

Years later, I gave it to a soapstone artist who finished it off beautifully, sold it and she was able to make a handsome profit. Although I didn't buy the finished work, I was pleased that she had completed my vision, and took it off my project list!

b) Blocking off time

Once you've identified the tasks you need to do, estimate how long each will take and jot that guestimate beside the task. Number them in order of priority, and get them done, one at a time. Start with the ones you might put off doing. It's best if you don't need to face them later in the day, when you're suffering from decision fatigue.

Try grouping like jobs together, breaking your schedule down into blocks of two-hour time slots, and slot in these times in advance. Then book the time in your planner like a 'real' appointment.

When you make an appointment to get things done, it's more apt to happen.

You have been gathering information to learn how to work more effectively. Keep searching for the right blend of tasks and new habits that work for you. It might be hard to swallow the fact that you can't get 100 things done each and every day, but that's the truth of the matter.

If you don't get all your tasks done, please do not be too hard on yourself. We all have inner voices that scold us when we don't accomplish everything we set out to do in a day. Tame those inner gremlins!

c) Rewarding yourself

Most people need more than just the satisfaction of getting the work off their plate. What kind of reward will help you do what you want to do? What's a good incentive for you to tempt yourself to accomplish a task?

How big or difficult is the goal? Choose a motivating reward.

Whatever you choose, remember you're the boss and you're the worker as well. How would you reward someone else for getting all these things done? Day after day, week after week, month after month, try to be as generous to yourself as you would be to someone working for you. Everyone needs to celebrate their successes, to feel appreciated to keep going. Running a business is a marathon, not a sprint. You need nourishment and cheering as you push yourself to keep going towards your goals. And, as in any long race, you need support people to help you stay the course.

"Time is a great teacher, but unfortunately it kills all its pupils."

Louis-Hector Berlioz
French Composer

CHAPTER 5

Kitchen Help or Delegating and Staffing

    a. The Work Plan Makeover
    b. Test and Measure
    c. How to Delegate
    d. Staffing or Team Management Pointers
    e. Staffing or Team Models

Chapter 5
Kitchen Help or Delegating and Staffing

a) *The work plan makeover*

After years of building a business, your passion for the work can suddenly fizzle. One day, you love what you do and it's easy to get up in the morning and do a good job.

The next day, you no longer feel the same passion for your product, service or client. You can't bring the same energy to promote your work. Sales start to fall off. While there may be parts of the business you still love, it could be time for a **work plan makeover**.

The concept of delegating work was introduced earlier in this book. The Job Satisfaction checklist introduced in chapter 2 will help you prepare for your work plan makeover. Once you create a running list of all the jobs that you do in a typical week and score them in terms of your enjoyment in doing them, from 1 (least) to 10 (most) you can create a plan to delegate, dovetail or delete those jobs you rated 5 or less.

Even if you spend an hour figuring out how to delegate these activities, it will pay off in the long run.

On the subject of delegating, here are a few tips to keep in mind. There are short and long-term solutions to delegating. Do you have more time or money to put towards this effort? Identify the work to be done before you create your approach to this plan. Do not bring close friends into your office to work for you. Although it can be a good short-term solution, over time it almost always damages the friendship. It's always a good idea to be friendly, yet professional with people in your business, and set clear boundaries and expectations.

Resist the urge to become friends with your employees. Over time, friendship can blur a working relationship and introduce communication challenges, for example, around performance and salary reviews, and these can take significant time to resolve.

For couples, working and living together can be a tough road to travel. Most couples admit they don't have any time for chit chat and that the business becomes their 'everything.' If you work with your spouse, sibling or significant other, create distinct areas of responsibilities and work zones in the workplace. Write up formal job descriptions and do your best to stay out of each other's day-to-day business. Schedule regular check-ins or status updates as a team. And set up some down time away from the business to feed your personal connection.

Interview and Screening Tips

On the subject of staffing, here are some helpful tips. If you have not interviewed people before, ask a friend with experience in the process or a mentor to sit in on the interviews to provide another point of view. This is important when you are considering several excellent candidates.

1. Interview at least a couple of people for any position
2. Meet them on the same day, if possible
3. Ask them open-ended questions to hear their stories
4. Ask their hourly fee and when they can start
5. Ask for and follow up with two references
6. Ask the referees open-ended questions about the candidate's service or performance (rather than "Were you

satisfied with..." ask "How satisfied were you with this person's ability to follow through on..."
7. Have the qualified candidates do a skills test of some sort related to your business needs (there are many online providers of skills testing and assessment)
8. For longer projects, you may want to engage someone for a probationary period of a few weeks or months to ensure a good fit
9. Offer the candidate a short-term contract, to be reviewed in 3-6 months

Delegating has served many business owners well. Once they build in support, they are freed up to do the higher-level work and earn more money, which easily pays for the support they require. It works best when they delegate work that they don't enjoy doing.

The next consideration is which activities can be dovetailed? You'll have rated some jobs at 5 or less because they are just plain boring!

Sepp, a computer programmer I worked with, taught himself to juggle while monitoring his pilot programs. He had to keep one eye on the screen and that was perfect for learning to juggle. Other activities, like filing can be enriched by listening to a TED Talk lecture or audio business book. If you are a speaker or make presentations, you can send your handouts to a copy shop via e-mail and pick up the finished products when you are out that way, or have an assistant, cab or courier bring them to you.

Finally, ask yourself which activities can be deleted. Take a fresh look not only at what you're doing but how you're doing it. Every day, technology changes the tools of your trade. Does your company letterhead still list your fax number even though you scan documents and email them? Do you still keep audio cassettes of a speaker you heard years ago? How dated are your industry trade indexes? You don't need to save those business cards, once you are connected with your new contacts via social media. Clearing outdated supplies out of your office helps you manage clutter and create space.

When I was helping Brian, a busy realtor client, one look at his storage cabinet let me know he had supplies that he could easily dispose of. When I asked about new equipment, I found out that he had recently replaced a printer. We were able to pull out all the ink cartridges for the old printer and called a recycling place that could use them. It was a good maintenance tip for his support team, who promised to go through the cabinet with fresh eyes.

You won't be able to delegate every unsavoury job. But you can reward yourself for getting them done in a condensed period of time with some motivation like lunch out with a friend or colleague.

Doing more of what you love to do will boost your income and add life to your years!

b) *Test and Measure*

Once you have considered a work makeover plan, it is important to test and measure when implementing the plan.

Begin this process by asking yourself: Do you know what you're good at doing, as well as what you like to do? It's not always the same thing.

Client Story

Gina made a line of plaster plaques for homes and gardens. She enjoyed doing the research and coming up with unique designs that captured people's imaginations. Through her website, she sold product online as well as at shows. However, being extremely shy, she returned home drained and needed to rest for up to a week. Gina called me in to plan her production space more effectively so she could hire someone to do all her shipping. She had part-time help on the production side, but needed to get out to stores and sell more. She was very uncomfortable doing this, so I suggested working with an agent. We re-worked her pricing and the first agent she approached was open to representing her line.

The next time she called me, the agent was driving her crazy with so many orders. We realized that her real love was the research and designing of new products. What she really needed was to hire more people for the production side of her business. Stepping away from production and delegating to staff was a delicate balance that she mastered over time.

c) How to Delegate

No one has a natural ability to delegate work. Delegating is a skill that you need to practice to learn. In your head, you know what you mean when you describe what needs to be done to finish the job you are describing. You might believe that 'everyone knows' what the finished product or project should look like, so you feel you don't need to spell it out. That is not the case. There are several ways to slice and dice. Some are more effective than others. The people you are delegating to cannot read your mind. You need to give instructions clearly and repeat as necessary.

An Operations Manual for your company is essential to manage your business effectively. It spells out the specific steps for your common business processes and administrative tasks. Having a manual helps you maintain better quality and control, and shortens the learning curve for new staff.

If you're just getting started on a manual, begin by opening a document on your computer. Ask each individual who successfully completes a job for you to write up the steps involved for the Operations Manual. Review the steps to make sure they're complete and clear, then add them to your document. Put them into a binder for easy access when you're training a new person. (Or add them to your Employee Orientation binder as your staff grows.)

Your operations manual makes delegating a job the second time much easier. Ask the new person to read these instructions and check whether they have any questions. Or, walk through the instructions with them to ensure they grasp the sequence of the steps. Plan check-in points with them; clarify your expectations regarding deadlines and quality, and follow up with them upon completion of projects.

You can become quite good at delegating work in your business and not do as well when delegating at home. I learned that lesson first-hand. I was under a deadline leading a team at work, when I asked my children aged 10 and 14 to make dinner. I was grateful for their support and reminded them to balance the food groups. Too little information! The children met the requirements—technically—and were thrilled with their meal: hot dogs and corn on the cob. I thanked them and laughed at my mistake as I sliced up a tomato and talked about adding color to each meal.

Strings Attached

It's easier to understand how to delegate well when you think of it in terms of passing along work with 'strings attached,' that is, instructions.

When you begin to delegate, there's a natural tendency to give too few instructions and delegate lots of responsibility without thinking things through. You may believe there is only one way to do the job, or you fail to clarify timelines or how this specific task fits into the overall working of your operations plan.

Once you're been burned, it's easier to feel that it's easier to just do the job yourself. I hear that from business owners often. That plan does not allow your business to grow.

Whenever you delegate, describe what the specific goal is and paint a picture of the finished job. For example, "This white paper will help our prospects understand how we can help them." After you outline the project, ask the other person to describe the goal in their own words.

Checkpoints

Decide or agree on your first check-in point. When and what will the person send you when they get to that check-in stage? Clarify when you would like the first check-in to happen, in a couple of hours or a couple of days? This first checkpoint allows you to make sure they are on the correct path. It also allows them to ask questions now that they are a little further into the project.

Once you have given your instructions, ask if they have any questions, need more information, and understand the direction of the project they are undertaking. For example, you could pose the question "Do you feel that you understand what our prospects are looking for–and how our company can help them find it?"

If it's a complex project, ensure that there are a few checkpoints along the way. You may need to revise the direction or refine the process. It's up to you, the 'delegator' to keep the project on track.

If time allows, let the person who is doing the work complete the job. Resist the temptation to take over at the first snag. Challenges help us get information to do a better job the next time. They will also have the satisfaction of completing the work.

Different Strokes

Be patient. Yes, you could do this job faster, but it took you a long while to get this good at this type of work. Soon your support person will be up to speed, and you are still free to do other work.

Stay calm. Yes, you could do this job better; but for many jobs, B+ is enough. If you continue to do everything, you will not get to do those more important jobs. And believe me, more satisfying work awaits you!

Reinforce achievement. Remember to offer encouragement along the way and some positive reinforcement when your employee, intern or student has completed the project. Yes, you pay people for their efforts, but people yearn for something else. Kindness, recognition and appreciation mean the world to people and are often more meaningful than the money you can offer them.

Build trust. Once you have delegated a few projects to the same person, you will learn to trust one another and to check in along the way in a casual manner. This person can become quite valuable to your business; make it a point to recognize them in meaningful ways.

Don't assume that learning curves are the same for everyone. When you begin to delegate to a new hire, subcontractor, student, nanny, etc., go back to the beginning of the process or job. Different people have different learning and working styles. Check your assumptions of their understanding again. Yes, they have the Operations Manual, but spot-check their work.

Re-focus after you delegate. Each person you engage can support you and your business in a variety of ways. This allows you to focus on what you're good at and what you love to do.

d) Staffing or team management pointers

When you work with a team or staff, it's important to meet regularly with them. Put a weekly or monthly team meeting in place. If you have an assistant or right-hand person, meet with them more regularly than others, face-to-face, by phone or text. Touch base daily with someone as they begin to work with you. This ensures that each of you knows what's going on. Some people choose to do this via e-mail or on the phone; some meet in person. You can review the lists for the day and delegate, dovetail or re-focus the day to maximize your results. Once you have some systems in place, you can meet less often.

For example, if one of you is going to the bank on the way to the office and the other needs something nearby, it saves travel time to dovetail those tasks. You can also remind each other of any overlooked details. A short call or text can save time every day. What would you do with an extra hour?

As you begin to work well together, you can shift to less frequent meetings. A couple of my clients have moved to instant or text messaging throughout the day. This does not work for everyone and can lead to a fractured focus, but can be invaluable for keeping everyone up to date on fast-changing situations. Plan to meet with your key staff or team members on a weekly basis. Planning time pays off in saving time and building synergies so you all get more done.

Meet with other team members in a group on a weekly or bi-weekly basis. Share an agenda ahead of time to ensure a tightly run meeting. This short meeting allows you to keep everyone informed and focused on the goals of your group.

If it seems impossible for you to meet with your team, ask for weekly or monthly reports to keep you in the loop. Ask for a one-page update from each person at the end of the week or month that summarizes what they accomplished or dealt with in that time. Create a template like the one below with open-ended questions to get at the information you require.

Company _____

Name_____ Date _____

Timeframe _____

What did you achieve/accomplish this week/month?

What was challenging for you this week/month?

What support do you require in the coming week/month?

What's coming up for you next week/month/quarter?

What new ideas did you consider this week or want to share with others?

e) Staffing or Team Models

Traditional employment models are not always an ideal match for a growing company as staffing needs can quickly shift. Using short-term contractors can be a better and less expensive option for you as you build your business. You can maintain a stronger and more flexible team by using part-time or independent contractors. Having your right-hand support person off sick or away from work has a much bigger impact than being short one of two part-time people. Many jobs require very different skills. It's useful to have a technical person doing the work they're good at doing, and a people-person handling customer service or staffing tasks. Check with your government regulations to conform to your local employment laws.

Virtual Assistance

Virtual assistance or virtual assistants (VAs) work out of their own office, use their own equipment, and serve several companies at once. Working anywhere, they work in a timely manner and communicate or deliver work via email, courier or post. Some clients who use this option have never even met their biggest support team members!

VA rates can be a little higher than hiring someone to work in your office, but can still be the wiser choice. Some VAs will bill in 15-minute increments, which can save you money in the long run. If you bring someone into your office to work with you and they wait for work to be delegated, it costs you money while they wait around. Some VAs offer different specialties: website updates, invoicing, administrative work, scheduling and travel plans, etc.

Sharing Workspace

Shared or co-working spaces are now a widely available option for different types of entrepreneurs from digital communications specialists to health care professionals.

The trick to finding a successful shared space option is to find a great location, a shared focus, and a set of 'house rules' you all uphold.

Is this a co-creative, inspirational, remote networking space, or just an address? With a shared focus, co-working or collaborative spaces can provide great opportunities for cross-marketing or spawn novel connections that lead to new business ventures.

How can you help a diverse, group of independent entrepreneurs work together effectively? If you have a healing clinic or counselling centre, for example, draw up an agreement to allow the other professionals to use the clinic to meet their own as well as the clinic's clients. Spell out costs, services, and shared responsibilities. For example, the center will promote and secure a qualified team to serve the clients they attract. Professionals such as an RMT, Reiki Master, Reflexologist, Acupuncturist or Psychologist could form a team to provide complete care to the patients of the clinic.

Client Story

An entrepreneur in recovery services worked with me over ten months to grow his dream business. At our first meeting, our goal was to reclaim his week-ends. He was working 'in the business' of counselling from Monday to Friday, and 'on the business' each week-end, preparing invoices and paying bills. He rented space in a doctor's office. At our first meeting, we dealt with his urgent need to reclaim some personal time.

As I prepared to leave that appointment, I asked him to tell me about his dreams for his business. He described a group practice that would be relatively easy to build. He was surprised to learn that I felt certain that we could establish that dream in under a year. We met each month and he took the necessary steps, one at a time. He currently oversees a practice that has five counsellors and other part-time contractors. They have a posh reception area, five offices and three group rooms that are booked by counsellors and other groups. His net expenses are about the same as he was paying as a solopreneur, but he has more income and flexibility. He has built in some passive income, works part-time and is able to travel regularly.

"If you don't know where you are going, you'll end up someplace else."

Yogi Berra
American Major League baseball catcher, manager, coach.

CHAPTER 6

Finding Your Perfect Recipe or Refining Your Recovery Plan

- *e.* Try Something New
- *f.* Test and Measure
- *g.* Refine Your Plan
- *h.* Your Personal Recovery Plan
- *i.* Annual Review

Chapter 6
Finding Your Perfect Recipe or Refining Your Recovery Plan

a) Try Something New

If you're reading this book in the traditional manner, then you've read over half this book already. You have collected a lot of new ideas. It does not serve you to simply collect ideas, without taking action on the ones that speak to you. It's time to take some action steps! It feels great to become an action hero! I had a sketch drawn of my face as Wonder Woman, and it proudly hangs in my office. When I need an extra boost of determination, I look there for inspiration.

Assess where there are still problem areas in your life. Where's your pain? Revisit your Lifestyle Audit to confirm. Identify what you want to work on. Check the index in this book to find the information you need. What idea is a good fit for you? What goal is worth pursuing? Are you considering?

- Working fewer hours per week (be specific)
- Arranging support for your work (what does that look like?)
- Setting up a better system at work (set a timeline)

What else do you want to accomplish? Again, be specific, be clear in what you need and set a timeline.

"Definition of Insanity: doing the same thing over and over again and expecting different results."

Albert Einstein
Theoretical Physicist

I feel certain that you've tried a few of the ideas presented in this book. What's worked? Have some of those habits stuck? You may want to refine your approach and try those habits again. Assess which new habits you'd like to adopt. Are there ideas that you feel certain will help you, but you can't seem to try them out to see if they would work for you?

If so, I'd recommend looking for an accountability buddy. See page 73 for details on getting an accountability buddy. You may be more motivated by sharing your goal with someone you respect. Share with a colleague the fact that you want to accomplish a goal or adopt a new habit, and ask them to check in with you on Friday. As a return favour, ask them if they have a goal or a daily habit that they would like to develop. Then both of you check back with each other at the end of the week and the next week, as needed. With support, anything is possible.

Identify what type of support you need. You don't have to do everything alone. Plan a new approach to a goal you want to accomplish or a habit you want to adopt. Find an accountability buddy and walk the path to reaching your targets together.

b) Test and Measure

It's important that you know what 'success' looks like to you. If you don't define specific measures or parameters around what success means to you, you may not recognize your goal when you've reached it. Assess your progress against your own measures and when you accomplish a goal, celebrate that milestone before you set out to reach a new goal. If you keep moving the finish line, you won't get the feeling of satisfaction of accomplishing things. Even crossing off goals from your to-do list can let you savour your accomplishments.

When you are feeling overwhelmed on some days, get out your highlighter and highlight each item you finish on your to-do list or in your day-planner. The completed items will pop out and you will feel great about the progress you're making!

c) Refine Your Plan

Benjamin Franklin said that *when you fail to plan, you plan to fail.* Even when you don't follow through on your plans right away, you understand where you're headed if you have a plan and know the steps you need to take. You'll get there eventually.

Have you tried using the Goal Chart (section 3.d) on a monthly basis? Is it a good fit for your working style?

Have you tested blocking off time in your daily planner for the plans you have already developed?

Have you found an accountability buddy, and tried a weekly check in with them?

Are there still things that you have to do or want to do to reach your goals, and can't seem to settle into doing them?

The Motivational Focus Program may help you stay on track. This idea has a high success rate when you know what you want to do. Set aside a block of time with someone whom you respect for their commitment to time and goal management. Three hours is the perfect amount of time for what I call my Motivational Focus Program (MFP). You will only use this time for those specific, challenging projects. Agree to speak once per hour and at the end of this block of time. For example, if you have blocked off 9 a.m. to noon for MFP, then work the time as follows:

9am – 5-minute chat stating what you will accomplish over the next hour

10am – 5-10 minute chat about how it went, and what you learned. State what you will do over the next hour

11am – another 5-minute chat about how it went, and what you plan to finish up doing

12pm – a wrap-up call to celebrate what went right and what you could do to accomplish more per hour (or MPH).

The Motivational Focus Program is my secret weapon when I come across something I want to do yet am procrastinating about doing it. My clients seek this fee-for-service option to increase their MPH (or more per hour).

d) Your Personal Recovery Plan

Use this section when you are ready to create your personal recovery plan to guide you to take the action you want to take.

WHY DO I WANT TO RECOVER?
IDENTIFY THE 3 TOP REASONS.

1)_____

2)_____

3)_____

HOW MANY DAYS DO I HAVE BEFORE I TURN 80 YEARS OF AGE?

_____ YEARS X 365 = _____

WHAT DO I WANT TO ACHIEVE BEFORE I TURN 80 or MY BUCKET LIST.

_____
_____
_____
_____
_____
_____
_____
_____

DO I WANT TO EXPERIMENT WITH A DIGITAL DETOX AND FIND OUT HOW IT FEELS? HOW LONG WILL I TURN OFF THE PHONE, NOT TOUCH THE COMPUTER AND STAY AWAY FROM THE COMPUTER?

_____
_____
_____
_____
_____
_____
_____

CLARIFY YOUR VALUES – CREATE A LIST OF THE 7 MOST IMPORTANT RELATIONSHIPS IN YOUR LIFE.
(Parents, Siblings, Children, Friends, Yourself, Life Partner, Business Contacts)

_____
_____

CLARIFY YOUR VALUES – AROUND OTHER THINGS.
(Business, Home, Entertainment, Health, Vacation, TV, Sleep, Food, Learning)

WHAT NEW HABITS DO I WISH TO ADOPT?

HOW CAN I PAIR THEM UP WITH A HABIT I ALREADY HAVE?

IDENTIFY THE ROCKS IN MY BUSINESS

_____
_____
_____
_____
_____
_____
_____

IDENTIFY THE ROCKS IN MY PERSONAL LIFE

_____
_____
_____
_____
_____
_____
_____

WHICH SELF MANAGEMENT TIPS OR TRICKS DO I WANT TO TRY?

(ie. False deadlines, plan my time in advance, using body language to influence people to leave my office, create a template for my week, plan a micro-vacation, become aware of what you do to procrastinate)

_____
_____
_____
_____
_____
_____
_____

WHO CAN I ASK FOR SUPPORT IN CHANGING THE THINGS I WANT TO CHANGE?

_____
_____

WHAT BUSINESS TASKS CAN BE DELETED?

WHAT BUSINESS TASKS CAN BE DELEGATED?

WHO CAN I DELEGATE TO?

WHAT BUSINESS TASKS CAN BE DOVETAILED?

OFFICE SPACE - HAVE I CLEARED OFF MY DESK?

HAVE I CLEARED OUT MY OFFICE AND STORAGE SPACES OF ANY BROKEN EQUIPMENT OR OBSOLETE SUPPLIES?

DO I NEED TO CREATE ZONES IN MY OFFICE?

DO I WANT TO TIDY UP EACH DAY OR ONCE PER WEEK?

WHAT PERSONAL TASKS CAN BE DELETED?

WHAT PERSONAL TASKS CAN BE DELEGATED?

WHO CAN I DELEGATE TO?

_____
_____
_____
_____
_____

WHAT PERSONAL TASKS CAN BE DOVETAILED?

_____
_____
_____
_____
_____
_____

e) Annual Review

Use this section on an annual basis, to remain aware of what you want to shift in your business and your life. Be honest with yourself as your answer these questions.

ANNUAL REVIEW (Write yes or no)

I plan my time in advance and cover the basics   _____

I delegate tasks that others can do well   _____

I'm happy on a regular basis   _____

I'm as healthy as I can be   _____

I'm feeling good about my eating habits   _____

I have friends outside of my business life   _____

I utilize my support people, to work less myself _____

I take time to teach others how to work 'in' my business _____

I create time to work 'on' my business _____

I understand my finances well _____

I plan for the future I want _____

My business helps me create the life I want _____

Address any areas that you have checked off 'no'. Build in the support you require to get where you want to be in your business and in your life.

> *"Let us not look back in anger or forward in fear, but around in awareness."*
>
> James Thurber
> *American cartoonist, author, journalist, playwright and wit.*

CHAPTER 7

Adding Another Course or Expanding Your Business

a. Hear a Need
b. Streams of Income
c. Taste Test
d. Workshops
e. Business Plans as Living Documents

Chapter 7
Adding another Course or Expanding Your Business

You may not wish to expand your business. You may want to relax and enjoy where you are right now. You may be reading this book to find more time for your personal life.

Yet there are ways to expand your business that can save you time while you earn more money. Does that thought appeal to you? The key to making this possible is to hire smart and trustworthy people to run the business for you. Have a system of checks and balances in place to know where your money is going. Sign your own cheques. When you run your business with fantastic people and keep track of the money, you will do well to expand your business.

Reach out to mentors in your field to learn how to broaden your own vision. Find out what has worked for them. What knowledge can they share with you? Research to find the right mentor for you and your business. You can contact me personally, and I would be happy to meet with you one-on-one or virtually. Give me a shout when you're ready!

a) Hear a Need

Listen—and you will often hear of a need for a new product or service from the clients you serve. They may ask you for a referral to someone or some product to solve a problem. You may respond with a solution and not think about it again. And you won't 'hear the need.' But if you capture these questions in a safe place, you may be able to identify the need for a new product or service you can provide.

Just write down these requests on scraps of paper and throw them into an 'idea jar' in your office or home, or file them under 'Needs and Ideas.' Later, sit down and read through them. You may begin to discern needs and wants that are common among clients. As you consider solutions for them, you may be able to develop new offerings for your clients and prospects.

Once you pare down your list of ideas, you can do the research and develop the product yourself, or pay someone else to develop it, and market it to your target audience.

b) Streams of Income

When you identify one need, do the research (or have someone do the research) to find out if there is a product or service already out there. You may find the perfect product that has already been developed. This is good news! Find out if your company can be a reseller of this product and offer it on your website. If it fits the need, bull's eye! You didn't need to take the time to develop the product, and now you've got passive income.

If the product has not yet been developed, brainstorm with a few clients to assess if it would sell well to your target market. Ask what they would pay for that product or service?

From experience, I know it is a treat to wake up to a few of those PayPal check marks in your inbox! You've literally made money in your sleep! This is a good thing. It allows you to grow your business while helping your overall cash flow.

Client Story

Farah had a doggie daycare and built a thriving business by developing a few streams of income. When asked to recommend a good dog-groomer in the area, she decided to invite one to rent a few days per week in the basement area of the building. The groomer set up the appointments and Farah got a cut of each appointment until the groomer had a strong enough business to pay regular rental rates. She also set up a small retail space for pet products in between the double gates necessary to keep the dogs safely inside. She began by selling simple handmade crafts and bought local handiwork, and later added a line of shampoos and doggie clothing.

Farah and her team took captivating photos of the dogs having a good time at daycare and sent them to the owners via e-mail during their workday. These photos were branded with her company name/logo. Her clients promoted her services when they forwarded these photos to their friends. It was a win-win situation. She then developed a dog-walking service for dogs who were not in her doggie daycare. Delegating a staff member and a co-op student to walk the dogs, she was able to walk double the number of dogs she could walk on her own. Eventually, she sold her business and became a dog services consultant.

c) Taste Test

Have you ever bought a product after you've tasted it in the grocery store? I sure have! Let me offer you another example of creating a second stream of income. If you are a web designer, your clients are probably asking for Search Engine Optimization (SEO). You could find a company that does SEO and ask if they would pay a "finder's fee" for the new clients your send them.

Or, you may choose to move into this field. You could begin by developing a tip sheet from research and information and assess their interest level for SEO. Then you could give them a 'Ten Tips for SEO' as a freebie when your service on their site is complete. You might also offer to do SEO at reduced rates for clients in good standing in their respective industries. This work may probably take time to do well, as you are learning a new skill or service. If your clients are pleased with your service, ask them to write a testimonial for the work. Ask them to tell others about your service. You may even want to offer them some additional services for each referral they give you.

Once you have cut your learning curve, you can develop a few SEO packages that would be worthwhile for your prospects and clients with new and established websites. You could offer special pricing to your own clients, as they are already onboard with your company. It's always easier to sell additional services to clients who already know you and your business. Their trust has been established.

If you give presentations to groups, your 'Tips Sheet' will make a great handout. It establishes you as an expert on the topic. Please ensure that it is well branded with your company information. The prospects in the audience may still hire you to perform that service. People often hire professionals to do a task for which they already have all the information to implement. It doesn't mean they will do the task themselves. Many prefer to hire others so they can 'buy back time' to do what they're good.

It can make business sense to give prospects a taste test of a new idea or service. They will let you know if they want more.

d) Workshops/Events

A great way to market your services is to organize a workshop or seminar for a mix of clients and prospects. Your workshop can bring everyone together in a physical space or an online forum. Survey a few of your best clients to find out which type of seminar format they'd prefer and find the common needs for their business. There are online tools like Survey Monkey that make it easy to get the feedback you require. Then develop your program to meet that need.

If there are a few things that you can't easily cover, invite another professional to present 10 minutes around that topic. You can cross-promote: ask the other professional to invite their prospects and clients to participate in the seminar.

You'll find that it's important to charge for this seminar. Free events are under attended. Even a nominal fee of $20 makes a difference to their commitment to show up. You can easily set up an online service like Eventbrite to sell tickets. You can also use Eventbrite at no charge to organize tickets for free events.

Physical vs Online Venues

Bringing people together gives them the chance to meet and network. The benefits of hosting events for only your clients include expressing your appreciation, letting them see who else you're working with, and making them feel part of an exclusive club. Bringing together prospects and clients usually gets you more clients!

You can usually book a meeting room in a local restaurant or rent a community boardroom or other public space. Decide whether you will charge a fee for attendance or put on the event for free as a marketing effort. Note that many free events are under-attended. People register, intending to go and then something comes up and they don't show up. Charging a small fee, even as little as $20, seems to help commit them to attend. Once they've bought a ticket, if they can't attend, they give their ticket to someone you might not otherwise reach.

Offering your workshop online saves travel time and extends your reach, as there are no geographic boundaries or travel considerations. It works well to offer this type of seminar free while it's live, and afterwards charge people a small fee to listen to the recording.

Develop a promotional e-mail and circulate it to measure the level of interest out there. Include a link to an online registration form so that people can register without any effort on your end. If you're working with another business owner, be clear on your expectation that they will promote the event through their networks.

At the event, present a program that helps the participants solve a problem or issue that they face. They see the value of your business to them. Follow up via e-mail or social media with a tip sheet or white paper to provide more reasons for them to become raving fans of you and your business!

The year I started this business, I rented a library auditorium and sold tickets to a business seminar called Small Office Strategies. Follow up from that seminar netted me a few clients and over 20 bookings for speaking events in the following year. It was well worth the effort. Speaking engagements were a significant part of my marketing plan for years.

To recap, here are the steps to consider when organizing events:

1) Choose a topic for your seminar, give it a catchy name.
2) Is it best suited for clients or clients and prospects?
3) Will it be in person or online?
4) Where will you host it?
5) Do you want to invite other experts?
6) Promote your event online and in traditional media.
7) What refreshments will you serve?
8) Put on an awesome event!
9) Will you sell or giveaway a tip sheet or booklet?
10) Follow up with prospects to maximize your efforts.

e) Business Plans as Living Documents

Once you have refined these presentations over time, you would add them as new products or services when you update your business plan. I update my business plans each spring. I see this season as a time for new growth and renewal. When I spot the buds on the trees and those brave spring flowers, I'm inspired to renew my business as well. Business plans act as maps toward the future of your business. It's important to treat your business plan as a living document. Revise it on a regular basis to keep it relevant to where you're headed.

When you review your goals, put in measures to assess your progress against those goals and reward yourself for achieving them. You can put in a reminder in your schedule to take a monthly micro-vacation. When you plan ideas and goals on paper, you see what needs to be done to make a living from this new aspect of your business.

> *"Success is not final; failure is not fatal: it is the courage to continue that counts."*
>
> Winston Churchill
> *Author and British Prime Minister*

CHAPTER 8

Reclaiming the Flavour of Life or Reclaiming Your Life

---

    a. Assessing NOW
    b. Power of Play
    c. Boundaries with Others
    d. Creating a Life Makeover Plan
    e. Finding Mentors

Chapter 8
Reclaiming the Flavour of Life or Reclaiming your Life

a) Assessing NOW

It's important to take time to 'Notice Our Worth' (NOW). We are the biggest asset in our business and our life. Our mental or physical health can suffer when we stop appreciating the good fortune that has already come out way.

Entrepreneurs are masters of delayed gratification. They put off savouring their successes, not realizing that this does not 'feed' their success. As you work hard to grow your business, delaying your own gratification can become a 'bad' habit. Once the business grows and surpasses the first set of goals, your attention immediately shifts to the next challenge. You are drawn to set more and new challenges to lead you to the next level. You can find yourself chasing your tail: to get the money to fuel the growth, you need to make more money. When it all becomes overwhelming, it is time to do some things differently.

STOP – for a moment. Ask yourself questions:

Where are you NOW? Where are you headed? Can you take a little time to play NOW? If not, can you block off time to think about what might be fun for you to do soon. If not now, when? Block off the time in advance, or tie a reward into a specific accomplishment. Are you going to work hard and play hard? Would you prefer to work smarter and then relax and recharge to do more of what matters to you?

Get some support at work so you can take time off NOW. Consider it as essential time to recharge and reflect, even if you can only spare time for a micro-vacation (4-24 hours), take time to reflect on where you are headed. Work on your recovery plan to lead you back on track.

b) *The Power of Play*

Play is undervalued in the lives of many solo/entrepreneurs. When you do take time to play, you realize how freeing it can be and the benefits of that break far outweigh the cost of working too hard over an extended period of time. When you play, your body relaxes, your mind wanders and you come up with some amazing solutions, or maybe you just escape the pressures of work for a while. This is a good thing. You return to running your business feeling refreshed. Trust me on this?!

Make a 'Creativity Date' with yourself. Go for a walk with a camera, and look for things that capture your imagination. Zoom in to take photos of things you would not normally consider capturing. If the weather discourages you, do something else creative with that time. Write. Play an instrument. Sketch. Sing. Dance. Paint. Make a stop-gap animation video with Lego. You get the idea? Play. It's not the results that count, but the process of letting go! Be creative and get away from it all for a bit.

There are some novel ideas mentioned at the end of this book. Try them to find s something fun that you'd like to do. If you've lost the urge to have fun, challenge yourself to try something completely different, and see what happens.

c) *Boundaries with Others*

People in my inner circle know that I often blur the boundaries with those closest to me. I say yes to almost any idea a close friend suggests. "Let's do it," I say! "When?" I suffer from 'Fear of Missing Out' (or FOMO) and tend to become overcommitted.

I wonder, "What if that concert is the best music ever? What if that party will be the highlight of the summer?" I could be asking myself, "What if I'm just trying to stay busy?" or "Do I need to take time instead to reflect on where I'm headed?"

As an extrovert who recharges in the company of other people, I feel the need to be with others after my workday. To balance my work and personal life, I block off one night per week to be at home to relax and do nothing. The reverse applies to my friends who are introverts; they take as much time as possible to recharge in solitude and try to force themselves out the door at least one evening per week.

The situation is different for each one of us as we have unique needs and circumstances. Developing boundaries around our commitments helps us reserve time for ourselves, our family and friends. Whenever we say "no, thank you" to a new idea or resist making a new commitment, and instead make time available for something or someone else that means more to us personally.

Having time for yourself and blocking off development time for projects that are important to you is critical to making life fun and worthwhile, and to making these projects happen.

Are you aware of your own boundaries? Take some time to consider what that question means to you in your own unique situation. Go to a coffee shop, get yourself your favourite beverage, ponder on and write down some thoughts about your own style.

One client shared that he was having trouble taking time out for himself when there was so much to be done for the business. We brainstormed and came up with a plan for him to take a Philosophy class. This would block off time for some reflection—

a topic of interest to him. He registered for a course and it was cancelled the night before it was to begin. He decided that he would try one evening of self-care and reflection at home. This has become a part of his regular routine and one that he values.

d) Add a Dash of Fun

What do you want more of in your life? People often find they have a list on the tip of their tongue in answer to this question: more fun, more time with friends, more romance, or more free time. You must consciously open up time to make room for these things that you have identified as core needs.

Whatever you focus on, GROWS. If you want more of something, focus on it. More fun? Make a list of things you feel would be fun to do, and then make a plan to do them. Start small. Once you experience the satisfaction from that 'fun' activity, you might be more willing to stretch yourself to make more room for these activities. This is a practical exercise. Pretend you are looking for more fun. Mull over these ideas and personalize the list below:

These are things that are fun to do:
More laughter
Funny movies
Comedy clubs
Time away with friends...
Date night with partner/family night/shopping with children

Once you have generated your personal list, choose one or two things to schedule in your planner for next month. Get a few successes with these items under your belt and as you enjoy yourself, you will be motivated to include more fun (for you) activities. For example, you may spot a hotel getaway deal nearby and call a friend to find out if they are interested in joining you. It's fun to plan an escape with a friend--even if it's only for 24 hours.

The best way to get more quality time with the people you enjoy being with is to reach out and invite them. For example, ask a close friend to choose a day near their birthday and plan a mystery date for them. Plan activities that you both enjoy and have fun with this 'day off.' Avoid appointments or paying for things in advance, as the day and plan works best if it is spontaneous and flexible. Make a reservation, but one that you can call to cancel.

You can start your day with breakfast at a local diner, where you lay out your plans for the day, letting your friend know that you can alter them if needed. You might select places they may not have visited that are free or low cost. If there is something that does not appeal to them, stress that it's their special day, and you can do something completely different. The only stipulation is that you spend the day together doing things that they (the friend) enjoys. It's fun to play tourist in your own city.

I've had some magical times with friends where everything seemed to fall into place to show us a good time. On one occasion, it was overcast as we moved between locations, and it rained almost every time we went indoors. Perfect! Another time, we met a busker who was making balloon animals. We got a kick out of those!

The nice thing is that you will enjoy these special one-on-one times as much as your friends! And, they will feel spoiled and know that they are 'special' to you.

Alternatively, you can mastermind a 'mystery date' to celebrate a friend or loved one. Send out a group e-mail, outlining the idea and ask people for a block of time that works for them. Each friend would take a two-hour slot, and meet up in a coffee shop or library and then pass the person being celebrated along to the next/new friend. For example: say: "I'll pick up Suzanne, take her to my favorite breakfast place, go shopping at that brand new store, and meet you at the coffee shop around noon. You can then take her out for lunch, and walk to the Art Gallery or a Yoga Class or some other activity that she loves to do. Find out who else knows what Suzanne has been putting off makes the options more entertaining for her. Whatever you focus on, GROWS. You can create a day that celebrates Suzanne and the things she loves to do!

Client Story

Years ago, I was working with a client in his office when he was called away to deliver something. His wife came into the office while he was gone and said "You've got to help him spend more time with us." When he returned, I asked him about the photos he had on his desk. He admitted that he used to travel extensively with his family. I admired a photo of his child and asked how old his son was now. He said it was a very old photo and his son was now 16. I asked if his son would still travel with the family. He said yes, but told me that he didn't feel that he could leave his business these days.

I helped him see that travelling with his son would be a time-limited offer as the son would probably not be 'delighted' to travel with his family in a few years. We worked together to make sure his business was maintained while he took a short trip to join his family on their longer version of a vacation. Everyone was thrilled that Dad would take some time away to join in the family holiday.

e) Finding Mentors

Mentors are vitally important to our lives and our businesses. Can you remember your early mentors? Often they were family members, teachers or early bosses. We think fondly of the first person who we felt *really* believed in us. These people may be surprised to learn that you considered them a mentor.

List these early mentors:

_____

_____

_____

_____

_____

_____

_____

_____

_____

Are these early mentors still available to you? Do you still ask them for their opinion/advice?

When you are open to learning from others, you will discover many mentors. They are out there, waiting to be asked for their opinion. Consider who is further along in your line of business. Whose success in business matches your vision for your own business? That individual may make a good mentor for you. They may not see you or your company as a threat, and you can bet that they were given a hand up along the way, so they may be ready to pay it forward.

If the competition factor makes this a tricky option for you, consider a business model that is close to yours and in a somewhat different industry. For example, someone in a cookie-making company might turn to a candy manufacturer for advice and mentorship. They are each in the snack industry and have similar challenges with storage, shipping, food processing regulations, and so on, but they have different target markets for their end products.

You can have several mentors. That's how I prefer to work. I meet with several people one-on-one for lunch a couple of times per year.

A few of my mentors first met me when I called them up to ask permission to ask them ten questions over ten minutes about a specific challenge I was facing. They readily accepted a coffee meeting or a phone chat. These relationships grew in trust and confidence over the years. Some of my other mentors I already knew earlier and when I asked them for business advice, they were very willing to share their insights and knowledge.

When I finished writing my first book, I asked everyone I knew to recommend contacts who had published a business book. I drafted 10 questions that took an average of 15 minutes to ask and elicit a response. I made 10 new contacts through this exercise and learned a lot about publishing a business book. I also learned about self-publishing. So then I asked everyone I knew to recommend contacts who had self-published a business book. Through these new contacts, I decided that self-publishing was the way I would proceed with my own book. It turned out to be a smart way to begin this journey.

Potential mentors for your future. List them here:

_____

_____

_____

_____

_____

_____

_____

_____

_____

I find it helpful to list my mentors by area of specialty so I can readily find someone to consult with when I face a challenge in their area of expertise. This mentor list helps stimulate some ideas of who I can phone for any issue I'm facing. When I call, if they don't know or feel uncertain about advising on the issue, I'll ask them who they can suggest who might be able to help. That often brings a new contact when they offer me a contact name or an e-mail introduction. Occasionally, they will call that person or facilitate a meeting.

You can also use LinkedIn to find mentors. Use the search functions to locate people by their area of expertise. If the search reveals contacts of persons you know, reach out and 'link' with the person you know and request an introduction to your potential contact. You may be only one shared connection away from the perfect mentor! You can then invite your new contact out for a coffee or even ask them for 10 minutes on the phone. Have your questions ready and see where the conversation goes. A few of my most important mentors came to me as a result of cold calls. The worst thing that can happen? They say no, which is not an issue. There are many other people to approach!

Use the form below to list mentors for your future needs. Dig your 'well' of support in anticipation of future challenges. You will be pleased for this quick reference sheet when the issues crop up.

ONE HUNDRED MENTORS

Name	Area of Expertise	Contact

The Mentors Circle is a structured peer-mentoring model I developed over a decade ago. It is a guide for business owners to help them bring together mentors in a circle to brainstorm and problem-solve around specific challenges. Members meet each month and set goals for their individual businesses. They are motivated to meet those goals before the next meeting of the 'circle.' They apply caring pressure and humour to hold each other accountable to their targets and aspirations.

From my experience, I estimate that members of mentor circles accomplish half their assigned goals the week before each meeting. That is because you can often feel more accountable to others than you do to yourself. And that's okay. Gathering new ideas and accomplishing your goals is the aim with the Mentors Circle. It can be the support you need to get more done each month and is a useful tool to use as you grow your business.

My book *The Mentors Circle* outlines why and how you would start a group. You can obtain copies along with the agendas and templates at ***www.mentorscircle.com***

CHAPTER 9

Bite-sized Treats

or Treasured Moments

Chapter 9
Bite-Sized Treats or Treasured Moments

A digital detox can show you how liberating it is to unplug from all devices, even for just a bit. Years ago, I told a story about a family I knew who had the TV on all day. The first person up in the morning turned on the TV and the last person who went to bed turned it off. Everyone who was listening to me agreed that not only was this practice unnecessary, but it robbed that family of quality time.

That night, while I was turning off my computer and cell phone before bed, I had a lightbulb moment! Why was I keeping these electronic devices on throughout the day? Then I started to experiment with turning off these devices and expanded my digital-free time whenever I could. What a relief it has been to have some 'unplugged' time to relax and recharge!

A few of my clients have experimented with this practice as well. They report having uninterrupted conversations with the people they love and whose company they enjoy. These deeper conversations have helped build stronger and more interesting relationships. Their thoughts seem more focused after going through a digital detox. Some reported better sleep after a day unplugged.

Give a digital detox a try, especially if you feel the technology intruding on your private time. The first time I tried the detox, it was uncomfortable for me. I went from Saturday at noon till late Sunday night. I had to put a towel over my computer monitor to remind myself not to absentmindedly turn it on. I also put paper there to jot down the e-mails and reminders I wanted to remember to do later. Each time I challenged myself to go a little longer in the detox. Now I can occasionally hold out the whole weekend without my computer and with minimal cell phone time. The line from Monty Python's 'Flying Circus' *"And now* for something completely different." reminds me of their quirky humour which inspired me to see the funny in life. I think of that particular line as I approach something new or outside my usual routine. Shaking things up a bit, even when you're busy, keeps life interesting.

When you're trying to balance in a busy lifestyle that threatens to gobble you up, you may have to try a few different fixes to find the right fit. I have put together the following ideas that have helped me not only survive, but thrive in the busyness that is my life.

Make a conscious approach to balance what you do in your work. This will help you re-align yourself in your world. For example, if you spend most of your time in front of the computer, you will want to offset this sedentary time by doing something physically active. If you are physically active every day, you will benefit from meditative or other quieter pursuits, which rejuvenate your body. If your daily activities are repetitive, keep exploring new idea to create a vibrant life. If each day delivers something completely different, consider what you need to find your center of balance before the end of the day. Take time to 'regroup' and refocus on what you need to do, to meet your own needs.

Customize Some Treasured Moments

Some of the ideas mentioned in this book may speak to your own situation. You'll feel inspired to try out a few exercises.

Take a moment now to jot down a few things you might like to try in your own situation. Don't worry about the 'how to do' yet – just write down what particularly interests you.

Add some of your own ideas to the list. Come on… think of things that you used to love to do? Create your own 'treasured moments' wish list. Make it fun.

_____
_____
_____
_____
_____
_____
_____
_____
_____
_____
_____   _____

Now, choose one of the activities described below. Choose just one. Do some research on your choice of activity. You might look for a class or a special interest group or invite a friend or two to join in the fun.

Go to your planner/schedule and block off time to try out one activity. Just do it now, while you are caught up in the thought of getting away to try something new and interesting.

This exercise is a warm-up to spark your interest in getting more done in less time, so you can give yourself permission to take time to play!

Here are some fun activities that I call '*Treasured Moments*'.

Bask in a Bath

This simple luxury is easy to overlook in terms of its worth. When you close the door, dim the lights and light some candles, any bathroom can be transformed into a place to recharge. Music is nice, but salts or bubbles are necessary. If you have not done so in a while, block off some time to revisit this idea of indulgence.

Meditation

The wonderful thing about meditation is that you can do it on your own, anywhere, and at any time of day.

Through a series of guided meditations and workshops, and through reading, I've collected a number of recordings and meditations that are meaningful to me and keep my stress levels down. I tend to skip meditation when I need it most, and then I remember how much better I feel when I make it a priority. I have come to realize that a day with a restless meditation is better than a day without any meditation.

Get in the Game

There's bound to be a game you loved playing. Pull together a ball hockey game or book the local rink for some 'old-timer' hockey. Rope some friends into a soccer game at a local park or playing field. Dig out your bat, ball and mitt and get up a game of catch with a friend, your neighbours or kids. Tennis, anyone? Get up and get going.

Old Tunes

Music can transport you back to favorite moments and special summers. I have a folder of music on my computer that reminds me of happy times and I play it when I need a lift. Find some uplifting music of your own to become the soundtrack to shift your mood. Try dancing to release the tension in the muscles of your body. Nobody's watching so let yourself go!

Progressive Dinner Party

Ask a group of neighbours if they want to plan a progressive dinner party. Each one of you prepares (or buys) one course of the dinner, and you move from place to place.

Reiki

I learned of this 'energy' work through a friend. She had taken a weekend training and offered me a Reiki treatment, which felt pretty good. Then, a Reiki Master signed up for a business group I led. Once I experienced a treatment from her, I was hooked on the practice. The energy it gave me convinced me to study the mechanics of this treatment with her. I now treat myself on a regular basis. Experience a Reiki treatment to find out if it's a good fit for you.

Chuckle Belly

This simple idea gets everybody laughing. You need a bit of space and want to lie down on the floor. This is especially worthwhile for families. The first person lies down, and a second person places their head on the first persons belly and the third person puts their head on the second person's belly, and so on. There will be a chain of people lying down. The first person laughs at whatever they can, and the second person is guaranteed to 'catch' the laugh and pass it along. I've heard of children who ask their parents to "do Chuckle Belly" when things get tense. It lightens the mood.

Write Yourself a Love Letter

The longest relationship you will ever have is with yourself, and it's sure easier in this relationship if you can learn to love yourself.

A love letter writing workshop with Firefly Creative Writing helped me write a love letter to my brand new granddaughter which I hope she will save and one day understand the depth of my love for her. Our instructor encouraged us to write love letters to ourselves. I now keep a journal by my bed where I write to myself when I'm feeling grounded and special, and I read those entries on my 'off' days, when I need a boost.

Take Time Out

Turn off your cell phone and go for a walk. Reflect on what you would do if you had a 'free' day tomorrow. Really think about what you *want to do* when you have some free time.

Walk in a natural setting, whenever possible. The air is better and your thoughts flow freely when your brain doesn't have to be on alert as it is in the city. Walking helps getting more blood and oxygen to your brain. Scientists have proven that looking at nature alters the chemistry of our brains. Take a moment to contemplate the beauty in nature and daydream as you gaze at a tree or body of water.

Afternoon Movie

Really? Play hooky from work at an afternoon matinée?

Many moons ago, I was in another city on a business trip and a few meetings were cancelled. I had no desire to go sightseeing, so I chose to go to a movie. It was set in Ireland and was so absorbing that when I finally emerged from the theatre into the daylight, I did not know where I was. The movie had so transported me that I had to pause outside the theatre to remember which city I was in and in which hotel I had reserved my stay. I asked for directions to that hotel, and enjoyed an Irish stew for dinner. I'm reminded of that movie each time I sneak away to a matinée in my own city.

Laughter Yoga

This fun was developed by Dr. Kataria and has spread to 65 countries to date. An evening workshop was my first experience and after laughing the evening away, it felt like 100 pounds had been lifted off my shoulders. I tried another event before I signed up to become a Certified Laughter Yoga Leader. Now, I seize the opportunity to add Laughter Yoga exercises into any workshop. It lightens the mood of the audience.

House Swap

Need a vacation but short on cash? If you do your due diligence, house swapping may work for you.

Searching the "house swap" section on www.craigslist,com, I found a couple who wanted to be in my city while I was in theirs. We swapped. I stayed in their home in Vancouver while they were in mine in Toronto. We collected mail and watered plants while we stayed in each other's places. No need for a house sitter!

Revisit a Former Passion

Remember anything that you used to get excited about? I encourage you to consider finding something like that again.

A client told me that he loved being part of an Improv community 20 years ago. He had been single then, and left when the politics and in-fighting got to him. Through discussion, we realized that he had a family and friends and a supportive workplace now, and that he could return to enjoy the Improv scene without needing the community aspect of that group.

Sit in Silence

All day long you are besieged by tasks and priorities competing for your attention. It's a nice break to turn off the phone (really, turn it off!) and step away from your workspace into a quiet place. Find a place of worship or any other place where no one will ask for your time or attention; sit and worship the silence. Let your brain rest a while. The rewards can be immeasurable. If you can't find a perfect spot, get comfortable wherever you are and watch the clouds go by.

Have a fling

If you're single and at liberty to do so, a fling can wake up parts of yourself that you haven't felt in a long while. It will distract you from your business and open you to your feelings in new ways. It can be a roller coaster, but thrilling nonetheless!

Twister Board

When you're ready to share the joy, find an old Twister board and take it to a busy intersection. Lay it down on the sidewalk and offer the first move to someone else. Join in as soon as they have started the game. Encourage others to take a turn. You could even take a sign or simply call to others to share the fun of that timeless game. (Send me an e-mail when you're ready to head downtown, and I'll meet you there for some Flash Twister!)

Take a Train Trip

Park the car and take the train instead for a long-distance commute or out-of-town meeting. Lulled by the rhythm of the journey, your brain can come up with unique ideas and solve challenges that you can't seem to solve otherwise.

I get some of my best ideas enroute to a destination, looking out the window and daydreaming. I've done some of my most valuable writing on the train and have also had poems pop into my head.

Circus School

Have you always dreamed of running away to the circus? Juggling clubs and circus schools offer training that absorbs your mind and feeds your imagination. Always wanted to learn to ride a unicycle? Sure you can!

Go to a Slam Poetry Series

Much like concerts or lectures, there are performances of poetry in most cities. It's just a Google away! There are many readings and some open mics. Your creative juices will start to flow in this stimulating environment.

Magical Tricks

When was the last time you tried to master a coin or another magic trick? Maybe a card trick would suit your tastes? They all offer a welcome break from tedious cocktail chatter. There are tons of videos on the web. Take a look at a few and master one for the next time you are bored silly in a meeting. Impress them all. People of all ages love magic!

Dance, Dance, Dance

Hip Hop, Belly Dancing, Latin Dancing, Ballroom Dancing, Ballet, Tap Dancing? What do you want to try? There's a class for that. Just keep asking around at local dance schools or community centres.

What makes you Happy?

I wrote this on my bathroom mirror and it's an effective reminder to face each morning. Make time to consider this question. Be your own happiness coach. Figure out what helps you feel happy, and create the time and money to do it. Giving yourself permission to do more of what makes you happy may be your biggest barrier to happiness.

Creative Dates

There are life-drawing courses in nearby art spaces. If you used to draw, find a drop-in location to revisit that absorbing focus of drawing the human figure. I took three people to a local art gallery class and we had a wonderful time. At the end of our class, we discovered that the person with the least amount of training had the most realistic drawings!

Once in a while, I yearn for the creative headspace I enjoyed while my children were small and I made and sold crafts at fairs. When it gets intense, I set up a creative date with a friend. The process must be more important than the outcome for a creative date to work well; no pressure to produce something 'artistic.'

I arrange a time, gather what I have or go to the dollar store to splurge on a few things that might be fun. We've created a dream island out of Plasticine, made whimsical Christmas ornaments out of pipe cleaners, and painted note cards for the people we loved. I went out by myself another time, early on a spring morning and drew hopscotch grids outside storefronts and homes where people would appreciate it. I stopped at an inner-city park and drew some more and left the chalk beside the hopscotch. After a break for tea, I passed by to witness children picking up where I left off.

The real win came when I spoke to the store owners or people who owned those homes about what I had done. They were delighted and had stories about people with wide grins re-discovering hopscotch. One hairdresser went out and bought sidewalk chalk to reinforce the grid the following week.

Yoga, Tai Chi or Qigong

These activities each offer a chance to stretch your body and still your mind. This is a valuable combination for a stretched-to-the-limits entrepreneur! A video, workshop or private classes will teach you the basics and then you can practice anywhere and anytime. These activities can be easily enjoyed in a yard, nearby park, a hotel room or at the cottage.

Swimming

Swimming is a fantastic low impact, strong cardio exercise. It's cheap and cheerful too! You can swim for fun, fitness or relaxation, or join a competitive adult (or Masters) swim club. The discipline of training puts you in a good mind space and keeps you physically fit.

Running or Walking

Both running and walking benefit your mind and your body. I prefer to 'walk and talk' with friends. For many years, I've been walking different routes each week with another entrepreneur as a walking buddy. We explore different parts of the city together. We split the walk into two parts: personal and business updates and problem solving. We each get equal airtime, unless one of us needs a little more talk time.

Success and Gratitude Journal

I started my first success journal to track the small wins in my business as it grew. This journal became the 'currency' that paid me in the first year of my business. I write up the appointments that go really well, as they are a success even if I don't end up getting the business. I still write in my success journal each week. I've added "What I'm grateful for…" on alternate pages. This helps me record and remember things I take for granted: my health, a sunny day, a phone call from a long-lost friend. I'll re-read a few pages whenever I need to remember the positive things that are in my life.

Walk a dog

You don't need to own a dog to walk one! If you are a dog person, you already know a couple of dogs in your neighbourhood. Next time you meet them on the street, mention that you would like to join their owners on a walk one day. They may respond to this idea. If you feel that you could manage the dog after getting to know it a little better, offer to walk the dog for exercise or even care for the dog on an evening or weekend. Many dog owners will be grateful for this support.

Some people even 'dog share' with neighbours and everyone is happier (especially the dog!). The dog moves back and forth on a schedule and seems to get more attention than a one-family dog typically gets.

Take a Class or Workshop

You are the largest asset in your business and when you enrich your knowledge and skill set, the benefits transfer to your business as well!

Maybe you saw a night course or workshop that appealed to you, but you didn't know how you would fit it in with your other commitments. The odd thing is that you can. If you commit to a class, you can shift things around to make it work; it feels so good to do more of what you like to do.

I took a Blues Harmonica course that was a blast and university courses that helped me broaden my perspective. For almost a decade, I've been in a writing group that meets every second week and the feedback and experience has been considerable.

CHAPTER 10

*After Dinner Mint
or Epilogue*

Chapter 10
After Dinner Mint or Epilogue

Riding Waves and Running a Business

Didn't catch that wave quite right. Head over heels I go. My head hits the sand while my feet stick out of the foam. Sand and salt water bubbles swirl all around me. I sit up with a silly grin and feel like a kid on the shoreline. I stand up again and realize that I haven't had this much fun in a long while.

Waded out again into the surf on this sunny day. Caught the next wave, and surfed back to shore. What fun! As I'm wading back out, I feel the pull of the wave that brought me in, heading out to form a new wave. This wave crests as I decide that it's worth catching. Another long ride to shore on the crest of a perfect wave. Childhood memories flood my mind. So many wonderful days were spent on water.

Self-employment is a little like body-surfing. We must learn to recognize the subtle signs above and below the surface. We need to monitor the level of the ocean floor, which shifts constantly. We need to keep an eye on the changing landscape of the surface of the water and examine each wave that comes our way. There are many choices to make. Experience and intuition constantly guide me in making choices.

The next wave takes shape around me. There are conflicting pressures. There's a push, pull of water going in both directions. I feel another wave breaking on either arm. It crashes towards the middle and lifts me off my feet. It's an exhilarating feeling – *to be in the eye of a break in a wave.*

That last one really got my adrenaline going and made me want even more excitement. It's such an addictive drug, adrenaline. I swim out again, looking for a bigger wave. The satisfaction of riding each wave into shore is exciting!

There are as many options to choose from in this afternoon as I face each week in my business.

As I stroll along the beach afterwards,
I pick up a shell to remember this special day.
I'll make it into a necklace, and wear it when
I want to recapture this time.

The saltwater and sand are in every pore
of my body. It took days to wash all the sand out of
my scalp. The thrill of this trip came home
with me. It has recharged me to work in a more
focused manner on my business.
It has reminded me how much I enjoy
riding the waves and running my business!

For a current list of other resources please visit:

www.officementors.com

Order other books by Elizabeth Verwey
from the products page at:

www.officementors.com

Contact Elizabeth Verwey directly with your
questions or comments:

elizabeth@officementors.com

Made in the USA
Charleston, SC
07 April 2016